From October to Brest-Litovsk

From October to Brest-Litovsk

LEON TROTSKY

AUTHORIZED TRANSLATION
FROM THE RUSSIAN

ÆGYPAN PRESS

1919

TRANSLATOR'S NOTES:

1. In this book Trotsky (until near the end) uses the Russian Calendar in indicating dates, which, as the reader will recall, is 13 days behind the Gregorian Calendar, now introduced in Russia.

2. The abbreviation S.R. and S.R.'s is often used for "Social-Revolutionist(s)" or "Socialist-Revolutionaries."

3. "Maximalist" often appears instead of "bolshevik," and "minimalist" instead of "menshevik."

From October to Brest-Litovsk
A publication of
ÆGYPAN PRESS
www.aegypan.com

The Middle-Class Intellectuals in the Revolution

*E*vents move so quickly at this time, that it is hard to set them down from memory even in chronological sequence. Neither newspapers nor documents are at our disposal. And yet the repeated interruptions in the Brest-Litovsk negotiations create a suspense which, under present circumstances, is no longer bearable. I shall endeavor, therefore, to recall the course and the landmarks of the October revolution, reserving the right to complete and correct this exposition subsequently in the light of documents.

What characterized our party almost from the very first period of the revolution, was the conviction that it would ultimately come into power through the logic of events. I do not refer to the theorists of the party, who, many years before the revolution — even before the revolution of 1905 — as a result of their analysis of class relations in Russia, came to the conclusion that the triumphant development of the revolution must inevitably transfer the power to the proletariat, supported by the vast masses of the poorest peasants. The chief basis of this prognosis was the insignificance of the Russian bourgeois democracy and the concentrated character of Russian industrialism — which makes of the Russian proletariat a factor of tremendous social importance. The insignificance of bourgeois democracy is but the complement of the power and significance of the proletariat. It is true, the war has deceived many on this point, and, first of all, the leading groups of bourgeois democracy themselves. The war has assigned a decisive role in the events of the revolution to the army. The old army meant the peasantry. Had the revolution developed more normally — that is, under peaceful circumstances, as it had in 1912 — the proletariat would always have held a dominant position, while the peasant masses would gradually have been taken in tow by the proletariat and drawn into the whirlpool of the revolution.

But the war produced an altogether different succession of events. The army welded the peasants together, not by a political, but by a military tie. Before the peasant masses could be drawn together by revolutionary demands and ideas, they were already organized in regimental staffs, divisions, and army corps. The representatives of petty bourgeois democracy, scattered through this army and playing a leading role in it, both in a military and in a conceptual way, were almost completely permeated with middle-class revolutionary tendencies. The deep social discontent in the masses became more acute and was bound to manifest itself, particularly because of the military shipwreck of Czarism. The proletariat, as represented in its advanced ranks, began, as soon as the revolution developed, to revive the 1905 tradition and called upon the masses of the people to organize in the form of representative bodies — soviets, consisting of deputies. The army was called upon to send its representatives to the revolutionary organizations before its political conscience caught up in any way with the rapid course of the revolution. Whom could the soldiers send as deputies? Eventually, those representatives of the intellectuals and semi-intellectuals who chanced to be among them and who possessed the least bit of knowledge of political affairs and could make this knowledge articulate. In this way, the petty bourgeois intellectuals were at once and of necessity raised to great prominence in the awakening army. Doctors, engineers, lawyers, journalists, and volunteers, who under pre-bellum conditions led a rather retired life and made no claim to any importance, suddenly found themselves representative of whole corps and armies and felt that they were "leaders" of the revolution. The nebulousness of their political ideology fully corresponded with the formlessness of the revolutionary consciousness of the masses. These elements were extremely condescending toward us "Sectarians," for we expressed the social demands of the workers and the peasants most pointedly and uncompromisingly.

At the same time, the petty bourgeois democracy, with the arrogance of revolutionary upstarts, harbored the deepest mistrust of itself and of the very masses who had raised it to such unexpected heights. Calling themselves Socialists, and considering themselves such, the intellectuals were filled with an ill-disguised respect for the political power of the liberal bourgeoisie, towards their knowledge and methods. To this was due the effort of the petty bourgeois leaders to secure, at any cost, a cooperation, union, or coalition with the liberal bourgeoisie. The program of the Social-Revolutionists — created wholly out of nebulous humanitarian formulas, substituting sentimental generalizations and moralistic superstructures for a class-conscious attitude, proved to be the thing best adapted for a spiritual vestment of this type of leaders.

Their efforts in one way or another to prop up their spiritual and political helplessness by the science and politics of the bourgeoisie which so overawed them, found its theoretical justification in the teachings of the Mensheviki, who explained that the present revolution was a bourgeois revolution, and therefore could not succeed without the participation of the bourgeoisie in the government. In this way, the natural bloc of Social-Revolutionists and Mensheviki was created, which gave simultaneous expression to the political lukewarmness of the middle-class intellectuals and its relation of vassal to imperialistic liberalism.

It was perfectly clear to us that the logic of the class struggle would, sooner or later, destroy this temporary combination and cast aside the leaders of the transition period. The hegemony of the petty bourgeois intellectuals meant, in reality, that the peasantry, which had suddenly been called, through the agency of the military machine, to an organized participation in political life, had, by mere weight of numbers, overshadowed the working class and temporarily dislodged it. More than this: To the extent that the middle-class leaders had suddenly been lifted to terrific heights by the mere bulk of the army, the proletariat itself, and its advanced minority, had been discounted, and could not but acquire a certain political respect for them and a desire to preserve a political bond with them; it might otherwise be in danger of losing contact with the peasantry. In the memories of the older generation of workingmen, the lesson of 1905 was firmly fixed; then, the proletariat was defeated just because the heavy peasant reserves did not arrive in time for the decisive battle. This is why in this first period of the revolution even the masses of workingmen proved so much more receptive to the political ideology of the Social-Revolutionists and the Mensheviki. All the more so, since the revolution had awakened the hitherto dormant and backward proletarian masses, thus making uninformed intellectual radicalism into a preparatory school for them.

The Soviets of Workingmen's, Soldiers' and Peasants' Deputies meant, under these circumstances, the domination of peasant formlessness over proletarian socialism, and the domination of intellectual radicalism over peasant formlessness. The soviet institution rose so rapidly, and to such prominence, largely because the intellectuals, with their technical knowledge and bourgeois connections, played a leading part in the work of the soviet. It was clear to us, however, that the whole inspiring structure was based upon the deepest inner contradictions, and that its downfall during the next phase of the revolution was quite inevitable.

The revolution grew directly out of the war, and the war became the great test for all parties and revolutionary forces. The intellectual leaders were "against the war." Many of them, under the Czarist regime, had considered themselves partisans of the left wing of the Internationale, and subscribed to the Zimmerwald resolution. But everything changed suddenly when they found themselves in responsible "posts." To adhere to the policy of Revolutionary Socialism meant, under those circumstances, to break with the bourgeoisie, their own and that of the Allies. And we have already said that the political helplessness of the intellectual and semi-intellectual middle class sought shelter for itself in a union with bourgeois liberalism. This caused the pitiful and truly shameful attitude of the middle-class leaders towards the war. They confined themselves to sighs, phrases, secret exhortations or appeals addressed to the Allied Governments, while they were actually following the same path as the liberal bourgeoisie. The masses of soldiers in the trenches could not, of course, reach the conclusion that the war, in which they had participated for nearly three years, had changed its character merely because certain new persons, who called themselves "Social-Revolutionists" or "Mensheviki," were taking part in the Petrograd Government. Milyukov displaced the bureaucrat Pokrovsky; Tereshtchenko displaced Milyukov — which means that bureaucratic treachery had been replaced first by militant Cadet imperialism, then by an unprincipled, nebulous, and political subserviency; but it brought no objective changes, and indicated no way out of the terrible war.

Just in this lies the primary cause of the subsequent disorganization of the army. The agitators told the soldiers that the Czarist Government had sent them into slaughter without any rime or reason. But those who replaced the Czar could not in the least change the character of the war, just as they could not find their way clear for a peace campaign. The first months were spent in merely marking time. This tried the patience both of the army and of the Allied Governments, and prompted the drive of June 18, which was demanded by the Allies, who insisted upon the fulfillment of the old Czarist obligations. Scared by their own helplessness and by the growing impatience of the masses, the leaders of the middle class complied with this demand. They actually began to think that, in order to obtain peace, it was only necessary for the Russian army to make a drive. Such a drive seemed to offer a way out of the difficult situation, a real solution of the problem — salvation. It is hard to imagine a more amazing and more criminal delusion. They spoke of the drive in those days in the same terms that were used by the social-patriots of all countries in the first days and weeks of the war, when speaking of the necessity of supporting the cause of national defense, of strengthening the holy alliance of nations, etc., etc. All their

Zimmerwald internationalistic infatuations had vanished as if by magic.

To us, who were in uncompromising opposition, it was clear that the drive was beset with terrible danger, threatening perhaps the ruin of the revolution itself. We sounded the warning that the army, which had been awakened and deeply stirred by the tumultuous events which it was still far from comprehending, could not be sent into battle without giving it new ideas which it could recognize as its own. We warned, accused, threatened. But as for the dominant party, tied up as it was with the Allied bourgeoisie, there was no other course; we were naturally threatened with enmity, with bitter hatred.

The Campaign against the Bolsheviki

The future historian will look over the pages of the Russian newspapers for May and June with considerable emotion, for it was then that the agitation for the drive was being carried on. Almost every article, without exception, in all the governmental and official newspapers, was directed against the Bolsheviki. There was not an accusation, not a libel, that was not brought up against us in those days. The leading role in the campaign was played, of course, by the Cadet bourgeoisie, who were prompted by their class instincts to the knowledge that it was not only a question of a drive, but also of all the further developments of the revolution, and primarily of the fate of government control. The bourgeoisie's machinery of "public opinion" revealed itself here in all its power. All the organs, organizations, publications, tribunes, and pulpits were pressed into the service of a single common idea: to make the Bolsheviki impossible as a political party. The concerted effort and the dramatic newspaper campaign against the Bolsheviki already foreshadowed the civil war which was to develop during the next stage of the revolution.

The purpose of the bitterness of this agitation and libel was to create a total estrangement and irrepressible enmity between the laboring masses, on the one hand, and the "educated elements" on the other. The liberal bourgeoisie understood that it could not subdue the masses without the aid and intercession of the middle-class democracy, which, as we have already pointed out, proved to be temporarily the leader of the revolutionary organizations. Therefore, the immediate object of the political baiting of the Bolsheviki was to raise irreconcilable enmity between our party and the vast masses of the "socialistic intellectuals," who, if they were alienated from the proletariat, could not but come under the sway of the liberal bourgeoisie.

During the first All-Russian Council of Soviets came the first alarming peal of thunder, foretelling the terrible events that were coming. The party designated the 10th of June as the day for an armed demonstration at Petrograd. Its immediate purpose was to influence the All-Russian Council of Soviets. "Take the power into your own hands" — is what the Petrograd workingman wanted to say plainly to the Social-Revolutionists and the Mensheviki. "Sever relations with the bourgeoisie, give up the idea of coalition, and take the power into your own hands." To us it was clear that the break between the Social-Revolutionists and the Mensheviki on the one hand, and the liberal bourgeoisie on the other, would compel the former to seek the support of the more determined, advanced organization of the proletariat, which would thus be assured of playing a leading role. And this is exactly what frightened the middle-class leaders. Together with the Government, in which they had their representatives, and hand in hand with the liberal and counter-revolutionary bourgeoisie, they began a furious and insane campaign against the proposed demonstration, as soon as they heard of it. All their forces were marshaled against us. We had an insignificant minority in the Council and withdrew. The demonstration did not take place.

But this frustrated demonstration left the deepest bitterness in the minds of the two opposing forces, widened the breach and intensified their hatred. At a secret conference of the Executive Committee of the Council, in which representatives of the minority participated, Tseretelli, then minister of the coalition government, with all the arrogance of a narrow-minded middle-class doctrinaire, said that the only danger threatening the revolution was the Bolsheviki and the Petrograd proletariat armed by them. From this he concluded that it was necessary to disarm the people, who "did not know how to handle fire-arms." This referred to the workingmen and to those parts of the Petrograd garrison who were with our party. However, the disarming did not take place. For such a sharp measure the political and psychological conditions were not yet quite ripe.

To afford the masses some compensation for the demonstration they had missed, the Council of Soviets called a general unarmed demonstration for the 18th of June. But it was just this very day that marked the political triumph of our party. The masses poured into the streets in mighty columns; and, despite the fact that they were called out by the official Soviet organization, to counteract our intended demonstration of the 10th of June, the workingmen and soldiers had inscribed on their banners and placards the slogans of our party: "Down with secret treaties," "Down with political drives," "Long live a just peace!" "Down with the ten capitalistic ministers," and "All power to the Soviets." Of placards expressing confidence in the coalition government there were but three one from a Cossack regiment, another from the Plekhanov group, and the third from the Petrograd organization of the Bund, composed mostly of non-proletarian elements. This demonstration showed not only to our enemies, but also to ourselves as well that we were much stronger in Petrograd than was generally supposed.

The Drive of June 18th

A governmental crisis, as a result of the demonstration by these revolutionary bodies, appeared absolutely inevitable. But the impression produced by the demonstration was lost as soon as it was reported from the front that the revolutionary army had advanced to attack the enemy. On the very day that the workingmen and the Petrograd garrison demanded the publication of the secret treaties and an open offer of peace, Kerensky flung the revolutionary troops into battle. This was no mere coincidence, to be sure. The projectors had everything prepared in advance, and the time of attack was determined not by military but by political considerations.

On the 19th of June, there was a so-called patriotic demonstration in the streets of Petrograd. The Nevsky Prospect, the chief artery of the bourgeoisie, was studded with excited groups, in which army officers, journalists, and well-dressed ladies were carrying on a bitter campaign against the Bolsheviki. The first reports of the military drive were favorable. The leading liberal papers considered that the principal aim had been attained, that the drive of June 18, regardless of its ultimate military results, would deal a mortal blow to the revolution, restore the army's former discipline, and assure the liberal bourgeoisie of a commanding position in the affairs of the government.

We, however, indicated to the bourgeoisie a different line of future events. In a special declaration which we made in the Soviet Council a few days before the drive, we declared that the military advance would inevitably destroy all the internal ties within the army, set up its various parts one against the other and turn the scales heavily in favor of the counter-revolutionary elements, since it would be impossible to maintain discipline in a demoralized army — an army devoid of controlling ideas — without recourse to severe repressive measures. In other words, we foretold in this declaration those results which later came to be known collectively under the name of "Kornilovism." We believed that the greatest danger threatened the revolution in either case — whether the drive proved successful, which we did not expect, or met with failure, which seemed to us almost inevitable. A successful military advance would have united the middle class and the bourgeoisie in their common chauvinistic tendencies, thus isolating the revolutionary proletariat. An unsuccessful drive was likely to demoralize the army completely, to involve a general retreat and the loss of much additional territory, and to bring disgust and disappointment to the people. Events took the latter course. The news of victory did not last long. It was soon replaced by gloomy reports of the refusal of many regiments to support the advancing columns, of the great losses in commanding officers, who sometimes composed the whole of the attacking units, etc. In view of its great historical significance, we append an extract from the document issued by our party in the All-Russian Council of Soviets on the 3rd of June, 1917, just two weeks before the drive.

"*W*e deem it necessary to present, as the first order of the day, a question on whose solution depend not only all the other measures to be adopted by the Council, but actually and literally the fate of the whole Russian revolution the question of the military drive which is being planned for the immediate future.

"Having put the people and the army, which does not know in the name of what international ends it is called upon to shed its blood, face to face with the impending attack (with all its consequences), the counter-revolutionary circles of Russia are counting on the fact that this drive will necessitate a concentration of power in the hands of the military, diplomatic, and capitalistic groups affiliated with English, French, and American imperialism, and thus free them from the necessity of reckoning later with the organized will of Russian democracy.

"The secret counter-revolutionary instigators of the drive, who do not stop short even of military adventurism, are consciously trying to play on the demoralization in the army, brought about by the internal and international situation of the country, and to this end are inspiring the discouraged elements with the fallacious idea that the very fact of a drive can rehabilitate the army — and by this mechanical means hide the lack of a definite program for liquidating the war. At the same time, it is clear that such an advance cannot but completely disorganize the army by setting up its various units one against the other."

*T*he military events were developing amid ever increasing difficulties in the internal life of the nation. With regard to the land question, industrial life, and national relations, the coalition government did not take a single resolute step forward. The food and transportation situations were becoming more and more disorganized. Local clashes were growing more frequent. The "Socialistic" ministers were exhorting the masses to be patient. All decisions and measures, including the calling of the Constituent Assembly, were being postponed. The insolvency and the instability of the coalition regime were obvious.

There were two possible ways out: to drive the bourgeoisie out of power and promote the aims of the revolution, or to adopt the policy of "bridling" the people by resorting to repressive measures. Kerensky and Tseretelli clung to a middle course and only muddled matters the more. When the Cadets, the wiser and more far-sighted leaders of the coalition government, understood that the unsuccessful military advance of June 18th might deal a blow not only to the revolution, but also to the government temporarily, they threw the whole weight of responsibility upon their allies to the left.

On the 2nd of July came a crisis in the ministry, the immediate cause of which was the Ukrainian question.

This was in every respect a period of most intense political suspense. From various points at the front came delegates and private individuals, telling of the chaos which reigned in the army as a result of the advance. The so-called government press demanded severe repressions. Such demands frequently came from the so-called Socialistic papers, also Kerensky, more and more openly, went over to the side of the Cadets and the Cadet generals, who had manifested not only their hatred of revolution, but also their bitter enmity toward revolutionary parties in general. The allied ambassadors were pressing the government with the demand that army discipline be restored and the advance continued. The greatest panic prevailed in government circles, while among the workingmen much discontent had accumulated, which craved for outward expression. "Avail yourselves of the resignations of the Cadet ministers and take all the power into your own hands!" was the call addressed by the workingmen of Petrograd to the Socialist-Revolutionists and Mensheviki in control of the Soviet parties.

I recall the session of the Executive Committee which was held on the 2nd of July. The Soviet ministers came to report a new crisis in the government. We were intensely interested to learn what position they would take now that they had actually gone to pieces under the great ordeals arising from coalition policies. Their spokesman was Tseretelli. He nonchalantly explained to the Executive Committee that those concessions which he and Tereshchenko had made to the Kiev Rada did not by any means signify a dismemberment of the country, and that this, therefore, did not give the Cadets any good reason for leaving the Ministry. Tseretelli accused the Cadet leaders of practicing a centralistic doctrinarism, of failing to understand the necessity for compromising with the Ukrainians, etc., etc. The total impression was pitiful in the extreme: the hopeless doctrinaire of the coalition government was hurling the charge of doctrinarism against the crafty capitalist politicians who seized upon the first suitable excuse for compelling their political clerks to repent of the decisive turn they had given to the course of events by the military advance of June 18th.

After all the preceding experience of the coalition, there would seem to be but one way out of the difficulty — to break with the Cadets and set up a Soviet government. The relative forces within the Soviets were such at the time that the Soviet's power as a political party would fall naturally into the hands of the Social-Revolutionists and the Mensheviki. We deliberately faced the situation. Thanks to the possibility of reelections at any time, the mechanism of the Soviets assured a sufficiently exact reflection of the progressive shift toward the left in the masses of workers and soldiers. After the break of the coalition with the bourgeoisie, the radical tendencies should, we expected, receive a greater following in the Soviet organizations. Under such circumstances, the proletariat's struggle for power would naturally move in the channel of Soviet organizations and could take a more normal course. Having broken with the bourgeoisie, the middle-class democracy would itself fall under their ban and would be compelled to seek a closer union with the Socialistic proletariat. In this way the indecisiveness and political indefiniteness of the middle-class democratic elements would be overcome sooner or later by the working masses, with the help of our criticism. This is the reason why we demanded that the leading Soviet parties, in which we had no real confidence (and we frankly said so), should take the governing power into their own hands.

But even after the ministerial crisis of the 2nd of July, Tseretelli and his adherents did not abandon the coalition idea. They explained in the Executive Committee that the leading Cadets were, indeed, demoralized by doctrinarism and even by counter-revolutionism, but that in the provinces there were still many bourgeois elements which could still go hand in hand with the revolutionary democrats, and that in order to make sure of their co-operation it was necessary to attract representatives of the bourgeoisie into the membership of the new ministry. Dan already entertained hopes of a radical-democratic party to be hastily built up, at the time, by a few pro-democratic politicians. The report that the coalition government had been broken up, only to be replaced by a new coalition, spread rapidly through Petrograd and provoked a storm of indignation among the workingmen and soldiers everywhere. Thus the events of July 3rd-5th were produced.

The July Days

Already during the session of the Executive Committee we were informed by telephone that a regiment of machine-gunners was making ready for attack. By telephone, too, we adopted measures to check these preparations, but the ferment was working among the people. Representatives of military units that had been disciplined for insubordination brought alarming news from the front, of repressions which aroused the garrison. Among the Petrograd workingmen the displeasure with the official leaders was intensified also by the fact that Tseretelli, Dan, and Cheidze misrepresented the general views of the proletariat in their endeavor to prevent the Petrograd Soviet from becoming the mouthpiece of the new tendencies of the toilers. The All-Russian Executive Committee, formed in the July Council and depending upon the more backward provinces, put the Petrograd Soviet more and more into the background and took all matters into its own hands, including even local Petrograd affairs.

A clash was inevitable. The workers and soldiers pressed from below, vehemently voiced their discontent with the official Soviet policies and demanded greater resolution from our party. We considered that, in view of the backwardness of the provinces, the time for such a course had not yet arrived. At the same time, we feared that the events taking place at the front might bring extreme chaos into the revolutionary ranks, and desperation to the hearts of the people. The attitude of our party toward the movement of July 3rd-5th was quite well defined. On the one hand, there was the danger that Petrograd might break away from the more backward parts of the country; while on the other, there was the feeling that only the active and energetic intervention of Petrograd could save the day. The party agitators who worked among the people were working in harmony with the masses, conducting an uncompromising campaign.

There was still some hope that the demonstration of the revolutionary masses in the streets might destroy the blind doctrinarism of the coalitionists and make them understand that they could retain their power only by breaking openly with the bourgeoisie. Despite all that had recently been said and written in the bourgeois press, our party had no intention whatever of seizing power by means of an armed revolt. In point of fact, the revolutionary demonstration started spontaneously, and was guided by us only in a political way.

The Central Executive Committee was holding its session in the Taurida Palace, when turbulent crowds of armed soldiers and workmen surrounded it from all sides. Among them was, of course, an insignificant number of anarchistic elements, which were ready to use their arms against the Soviet center. There were also some "pogrom" elements, black-hundred elements, and obviously mercenary elements, seeking to utilize the occasion for instigating pogroms and chaos. From among the sundry elements came the demands for the arrest of Chernoff and Tseretelli, for the dispersal of the Executive Committee, etc. An attempt was even made to arrest Chernoff. Subsequently, at Kresty, I identified one of the sailors who had participated in this attempt; he was a criminal, imprisoned at Kresty for robbery. But the bourgeois and the coalitionist press represented this movement as a pogromist, counter-revolutionary affair, and, at the same time, as a Bolshevist crusade, the immediate object of which was to seize the reins of Government by the use of armed force against the Central Executive Committee.

The movement of July 3rd-5th had already disclosed with perfect clearness that a complete impotence reigned within the ruling Soviet parties at Petrograd. The garrison was far from being all on our side. There were still some wavering, undecided, passive elements. But if we should ignore the junkers, there were no regiments at all which were ready to fight us in the defense of the Government or the leading Soviet parties. It was necessary to summon troops from the front. The entire strategy of Tseretelli, Chernoff, and others on the 3rd of July resolved itself into this: to gain time in order to give Kerensky an opportunity to bring up his "loyal" regiments. One deputation after another entered the hall of the Taurida Palace, which was surrounded by armed crowds, and demanded a complete separation from the bourgeoisie, positive social reforms, and the opening of peace negotiations.

We, the Bolsheviki, met every new company of disgruntled troops gathered in the yards and streets, with speeches, in which we called upon them to be calm and assured them that, in view of the present temper of the people, the coalitionists could not succeed in forming a new coalition. Especially pronounced was the temper of the Kronstadt sailors, whom we had to restrain from transcending the limits of a peaceful demonstration. The fourth demonstration, which was already controlled by our party, assumed a still more serious character. The Soviet leaders were quite at sea; their speeches assumed an evasive character; the answers given by Cheidze to the deputies were without any political content. It was clear that the official leaders were marking time.

On the night of the 4th the "loyal" regiments began to arrive. During the session of the Executive Committee the Taurida Palace resounded to the strains of the Marseillaise. The expression on the faces of the leaders suddenly changed. They displayed a look of confidence which had been entirely wanting of late. It was produced by the entry into the Taurida Palace of the Volynsk regiment, the same one, which, a few months later, was to lead the vanguard of the October revolution, under our banners. From this moment, everything changed. There was no longer any need to handle the delegates of the Petrograd workmen and soldiers with kid gloves. Speeches were made from the floor of the Executive Committee, which referred to an armed insurrection that had been "suppressed" on that very day by loyal revolutionary forces. The Bolsheviki were declared to be a counter-revolutionary party.

The fear experienced by the liberal bourgeoisie during the two days of armed demonstration betrayed itself in a hatred that was crystallized not only in the columns of the newspapers, but also in the streets of Petrograd, and more especially on the Nevsky Prospect, where individual workmen and soldiers caught in the act of "criminal" agitation were mercilessly beaten up. The junkers, army-officers, policemen, and the St. Georgian cavaliers were now the masters of the situation. And all these were headed by the savage counter-revolutionists. The workers' organizations and establishments of our party were being ruthlessly crushed and demolished. Arrests, searches, assaults and even murders came to be common occurrences. On the night of the 4th the then Attorney-General, Pereverzev, handed over to the press "documents" which were intended to prove that the Bolshevist party was headed by bribed agents of Germany.

The leaders of the Social-Revolutionist and Menshevik parties have known us too long and too well to believe these accusations. At the same time, they were too deeply interested in their success to repudiate them publicly. And even now one cannot recall without disgust that saturnalia of lies which was celebrated broadcast in all the bourgeois and coalition newspapers. Our organs were suppressed. Revolutionary Petrograd felt that the provinces and the army were still far from being with it. In workingmen's sections of the city a short period of tyrannical infringements set in, while in the garrison repressive measures were introduced against the disorganized regiments, and certain of its units were disarmed. At the same time, the political leaders manufactured a new ministry, with the inclusion of representatives of third-rate bourgeois groups, which, although adding nothing to the government, robbed it of its last vestige of revolutionary initiative.

Meanwhile events at the front ran their own course. The organic unity of the army was shaken to its very depths. The soldiers were becoming convinced that the great majority of the officers, who, at the beginning of the revolution, bedaubed themselves with red revolutionary paint, were still very inimical to the new regime. An open selection of counter-revolutionary elements was being made in the lines. Bolshevik publications were ruthlessly persecuted. The military advance had long ago changed into a tragic retreat. The bourgeois press madly libeled the army. Whereas, on the eve of the advance, the ruling parties told us that we were an insignificant gang and that the army had never heard of us and would not have anything to do with us, now, when the gamble of the drive had ended so disastrously, these same persons and parties laid the whole blame for its failure on our shoulders. The prisons were crowded with revolutionary workers and soldiers. All the old legal bloodhounds of Czarism were employed in investigating the July 3-5 affair. Under these circumstances, the Social-Revolutionists and the Alensheviki went so far as to demand that Lenin, Zinoviev and others of their group should surrender themselves to the "Courts of Justice."

The Events Following the July Days

The infringements of liberty in the working-men's quarters lasted but a little while and were followed by accessions of revolutionary spirit, not only among the proletariat, but also in the Petrograd garrison. The coalitionists were losing all influence. The wave of Bolshevism began to spread from the urban centers to every part of the country and, despite all obstacles, penetrated into the army ranks. The new coalition government, with Kerensky at its head, had already openly embarked upon a policy of repression. The ministry had restored the death penalty in the army. Our papers were suppressed and our agitators were arrested; but this only increased our influence. In spite of all the obstacles involved in the new elections for the Petrograd Soviet, the distribution of power in it had become so changed that on certain important questions we already commanded a majority vote. The same was the case in the Moscow Soviet.

At that time I, together with many others, was imprisoned at Kresty, having been arrested for instigating and organizing the armed revolt of July 3-5, in collusion with the German authorities, and with the object of furthering the military ends of the Hohenzollerns. The famous prosecutor of the Czarist regime, Aleksandrov, who had prosecuted numerous revolutionists, was now entrusted with the task of protecting the public from the counter-revolutionary Bolsheviki. Under the old regime the inmates of prisons used to be divided into political prisoners and criminals. Now a new terminology was established: Criminals and Bolsheviks. Great perplexity reigned among the imprisoned soldiers. The boys came from the country and had previously taken no part in political life. They thought that the revolution had set them free, once and for all. Hence they viewed with amazement their doorlocks and grated windows. While taking their exercise in the prison-yard, they would always ask me what all this meant and how it would end. I comforted them with the hope of our ultimate victory.

Toward the end of August occurred the revolt of Korniloff; this was the immediate result of the mobilization of the counter-revolutionary forces to which a forceful impulse had been imparted by the attack of July 18th. At the celebrated Moscow Congress, which took place in the middle of August, Kerensky attempted to take a middle ground between the propertied elements and the democracy of the small bourgeoisie. The Maximalists were on the whole considered as standing beyond the bounds of the "legal." Kerensky threatened them with blood and iron, which met with vehement applause from the propertied half of the gathering, and treacherous silence on the part of the bourgeois democracy. But the hysterical outcries and threats of Kerensky did not satisfy the chiefs of the counter-revolutionary interests. They had only too clearly observed the revolutionary tide flooding every portion of the country, among the working class, in the villages, in the army; and they considered it imperative to adopt without any delay the most extreme measures to curb the masses. After reaching an understanding with the property-owning bourgeoisie — who saw in him their hero — Korniloff took it upon himself to accomplish this hazardous task. Kerensky, Savinkoff, Filonenko, and other Socialist-Revolutionists of the government or semi-government class participated in this conspiracy, but each and every one of them at a certain stage of the altering circumstances betrayed Korniloff, for they knew that in the case of his defeat, they would turn out to have been on the wrong side of the fence. We lived through the events connected with Korniloff, while we were in jail, and followed them in the newspapers; the unhindered delivery of newspapers was the only important respect in which the jails of Kerensky differed from those of the old regime. The Cossack General's adventure miscarried; six months of revolution had created in the consciousness of the masses and in their organization a sufficient resistance against an open counter-revolutionary attack. The conciliable Soviet parties were terribly frightened at the prospect of the possible results of the Korniloff conspiracy, which threatened to sweep away, not only the Maximalists, but also the whole revolution, together with its governing parties. The Social-Revolutionists and the Minimalists proceeded to legalize the Maximalists — this, to be sure, only retrospectively and only halfway, inasmuch as they scented possible dangers in the future. The very same Kronstadt sailors — whom they had dubbed burglars and counter-revolutionists in the days following the July uprising — were summoned during the Korniloff danger to Petrograd for the defense of the revolution. They came without a murmur, without a word of reproach, without recalling the past, and occupied the most responsible posts.

I had the fullest right to recall to Tseretelli these words which I had addressed to him in May, when he was occupied in persecuting the Kronstadt sailors: "When a counter-revolutionary general attempts to throw the noose around the neck; of the revolution, the Cadets will grease the rope with soap, while the Kronstadt sailors will come to fight and die together with us."

The Soviet organizations had revealed everywhere, in the rear and at the front, their vitality and their power in the struggle with the Korniloff uprising. In almost no instance did things ever come to a military conflict. The revolutionary masses ground into nothingness the general's conspiracy. Just as the moderates in July found no soldiers among the Petrograd garrison to fight against us, so now Korniloff found no soldiers on the whole front to fight against the revolution. He had acted by virtue of a delusion and the words of our propaganda easily destroyed his designs.

According to information in the newspapers, I had expected a more rapid unfolding of subsequent events in the direction of the passing of the power into the hands of the Soviets. The growth of the influence and power of the Maximalists became indubitable and had gained an irresistible momentum. The Maximalists had warned against the coalition, against the attack of the 18th of July, they predicted the Korniloff affair — the masses of the people became convinced by experience that we were right. During the most terrifying moments of the Korniloff conspiracy, when the Caucasian division was approaching Petrograd, the Petrograd Soviet was arming the workingmen with the extorted consent of the authorities. Army divisions which had been brought up against us had long since achieved their successful rebirth in the stimulating atmosphere of Petrograd and were now altogether on our side. The Korniloff uprising was destined to open definitely the eyes of the army to the inadmissibility of any continued policy of conciliation with the bourgeois counter-revolution. Hence it was possible to expect that the crushing of the Korniloff uprising would prove to be only an introduction to an immediate aggressive action on the part of the revolutionary forces under the leadership of our party for the purpose of seizing sole power. But events unfolded more slowly. With all the tension of their revolutionary feeling, the masses had become more cautious after the bitter lesson of the July days, and renounced all isolated demonstrations, awaiting a direct instruction and direction from above. And, also, among the leadership of our party there developed a "watchful-waiting" policy. Under these circumstances, the liquidation of the Korniloff adventure, irrespective of the profound regrouping of forces to our advantage, did not bring about any immediate political changes.

The Conflict with the Soviets

In the Petrograd Soviet, the domination of our party was definitely strengthened from that time on. This was evidenced in dramatic fashion when the question of the personnel of its presiding body came up. At that epoch, when the Social-Revolutionists and the Minimalists were holding sway in the Soviets, they isolated the Maximalists by every means in their power. They did not admit even one Maximalist into the membership of the Executive Committee at Petrograd, even when our party represented at least one-third of all the Soviet members. Afterwards, when the Petrograd Soviet, by a dwindling majority, passed the resolution for the transferring of all power into the hands of the Soviet, our party put forth the demand to establish a coalition Executive Committee formed on a proportional basis. The old presiding body, the members of which were Cheidze, Tseretelli, Kerensky, Skobeloff, Chernoff, flatly refused this demand. It may not be out of place to mention this here, inasmuch as representatives of the parties broken up by the revolution speak of the necessity of presenting one front for the sake of democracy, and accuse us of separatism. There was called at that time a special meeting of the Petrograd Soviet, which was to decide the question of the presiding body's fate. All forces, all reserves had been mobilized on both sides. Tseretelli came out with a speech embodying a program, wherein he pointed out that the question of the presiding body was a question of orientation. We reckoned that we would sway somewhat less than half of the vote and were ready to consider that a sign of our progress. Actually, however, the vote showed that we had a majority of nearly one hundred. "For six months," said Tseretelli at that time, "we have stood at the head of the Petrograd Soviet and led it from victory to victory; we wish that you may hold for at least half of that time the positions which you are now preparing to occupy." In the Moscow Soviet a similar change of leadership among the parties took place.

One after the other the Provincial Soviets joined the Bolshevik position. The date of convoking the Second All-Russian Congress of Soviets was approaching. But the leading group of the Central Executive Committee was striving with all its might to put off the Congress to an indefinite future time, in order thus to destroy it in advance. It was evident that the new Congress of Soviets would give our party a majority, would correspondingly alter the make-up of the Central Executive Committee, and deprive the fusionists of their most important position. The struggle for the convocation of the All-Russian Congress of Soviets assumed the greatest importance for us.

To counterbalance this, the Mensheviks (Minimalists) and the Social-Revolutionists put forth the Democratic Conference idea. They needed this move against both us and Kerensky.

By this time the head of the Ministry assumed an absolutely independent and irresponsible position. He had been raised to power by the Petrograd Soviet during the first epoch of the revolution: Kerensky had entered the Ministry without a preliminary decision of the Soviets, but his admission was subsequently approved. After the First Congress of Soviets, the Socialist ministers were held accountable to the Central Executive Committee. Their allies, the Cadets (Constitutional Democrats) were responsible only to their party. To meet the bourgeoisie's wishes, the General Executive Committee, after the July days, released the Socialist Ministers from all responsibility to the Soviets, in order, as it were, to create a revolutionary dictatorship. It is rather well to mention this, too, now that the same persons who built up the dictatorship of a coterie, come forth with accusations and imprecations against the dictatorship of a class. The Moscow Conference, at which the skillfully manipulated professional and democratic elements balanced each other, aimed to strengthen Kerensky's power over classes and parties. This aim was attained only in appearance. In reality, the Moscow Conference revealed Kerensky's utter impotence, for he was equally remote from both the professional elements and the bourgeois democracy. But since the liberals and conservatives applauded his onslaughts against democracy, and the fusionists gave him ovations when he cautiously upbraided the counter-revolutionaries, the impression was growing upon him that he was supported, as it were, by both the former and the latter, and, accordingly, commanded unlimited power. Over workingmen and revolutionary soldiers he held the threat of blood and iron. His policy continued the bargaining with Korniloff behind the scenes — a bargaining which compromised him even in the fusionists' eyes: in evasively diplomatic terms, so characteristic of him, Tseretelli spoke of "personal" movements in politics and of the necessity of curbing these personal movements. This task was to be accomplished by the Democratic Conference, which was called, according to arbitrary forms, from among representatives of Soviets, dumas, zemstvos, professional trade unions, and co-operative societies. Still, the main task was to secure a sufficiently conservative composition of the Conference, to dissolve the Soviets once for all in the formless mass of democracy, and, on the new organizational basis, to gain a firm footing against the Bolshevik tide.

Here it will not be out of place to note, in a few words, the difference between the political role of the Soviets and that of the democratic organs of self-government. More than once, the Philistines called our attention to the fact that the new dumas and zemstvos elected on the basis of universal suffrage, were incomparably more democratic than the Soviets and were more suited to represent the population. However, this formal democratic criterion is devoid of serious content in a revolutionary epoch. The significance of the Revolution lies in the rapid changing of the judgment of the masses, in the fact that new and ever new strata of population acquire experience, verify their views of the day before, sweep them aside, work out new ones, desert old leaders and follow new ones in the forward march. During revolutionary times, formally democratic organizations, based upon the ponderous apparatus of universal suffrage, inevitably fall behind the development of the political consciousness of the masses. Quite different are the Soviets. They rely immediately upon organic groupings, such as shop, mill, factory, volost, regiment, etc. To be sure, there are guarantees, just as legal, of the strictness of elections, as are used in creating democratic dumas and zemstvos. But there are in the Soviet incomparably more serious, more profound guarantees of the direct and immediate relation between the deputy and the electors. A town-duma or zemstvo member is supported by the amorphous mass of electors, which entrusts its full powers to him for a year and then breaks up. The Soviet electors remain always united by the conditions of their work and their existence; the deputy is ever before their eyes, at any moment they can prepare a mandate to him, censure him, recall or replace him with another person.

If during the revolutionary month preceding the general political evolution expressed itself in the fact that the influence of the fusionist parties was being replaced by a decisive influence of the Bolsheviki, it is quite plain that this process found its most striking and fullest expression in the Soviets, while the dumas and zemstvos, notwithstanding all their formal democratism, expressed yesterday's status of the popular masses and not today's. This is exactly what explains the gravitation toward dumas and zemstvos on the part of those parties which were losing more and more ground in the esteem of the revolutionary class. We shall meet with the same question, only on a larger scale, later, when we come to the Constituent Assembly.

The Democratic Conference

*T*he Democratic Conference, called by Tseretelli and his fellow-combatants in mid-September, was totally artificial in character, representing as it did a combination of Soviets and organs of self-government in a ratio calculated to secure a preponderance of the fusionist parties. Born of helplessness and confusion, the Conference ended in a pitiful fiasco. The professional bourgeoisie treated the Conference with the greatest hostility, beholding in it an endeavor to push the bourgeoisie away from the positions it had approached at the Moscow Conference. The revolutionary proletariat, and the masses of soldiers and peasants connected with it, condemned in advance the fraudulent method of calling together the Democratic Conference. The immediate task of the fusionists was to create a responsible ministry. But even this was not achieved. Kerensky neither wanted nor permitted responsibility, because this was not permitted by the bourgeoisie, which was backing him. Irresponsibility towards the organs of the so-called democracy meant, in fact, responsibility to the Cadets and the Allied Embassies. For the time being this was sufficient for the bourgeoisie. On the question of coalition the Democratic Conference revealed its utter insolvency: the votes in favor of a coalition with the bourgeoisie slightly outnumbered those against the coalition; the majority voted against a coalition with the Cadets. But with the Cadets left out, there proved to be, among the bourgeoisie, no serious counter-agencies for the coalition. Tseretelli explained this in detail to the conference. If the conference did not grasp it, so much the worse for the conference. Behind the backs of the conference, negotiations were carried on without concealment with the Cadets, whom they had repudiated, and it was decided that the Cadets should not appear as Cadets, but as "Social workers." Pressed hard on both right and left, the bourgeois democracy tolerated all this dickering, and thereby demonstrated its utter political prostration.

From the Democratic Conference a Soviet was picked, and it was decided to complete it by adding representatives of the professional elements; this Pre-Parliament was to fill the vacant period before the convocation of the Constituent Assembly Contrary to Tseretelli's original plan, but in full accord with the plans of the bourgeoisie, the new coalition ministry retained its formal independence with regard to the Pre-Parliament. Everything together produced the impression of a pitiful and impotent creation of an office clerk behind which was concealed the complete capitulation of the petty bourgeois democracy before the professional liberalism which, a month previously, had openly supported Korniloff's attack on the Revolution. The sum total of the whole affair was, therefore, the restoration and perpetuation of the coalition with the liberal bourgeoisie. No longer could there be any doubt that quite independently of the make-up of the future Constituent Assembly, the governmental power would, in fact, be held by the bourgeoisie, as despite all the preponderance given them by the masses of the people the fusionist parties invariably arrived at a coalition with the Cadets, deeming it impossible, as they did, to create a state power without the bourgeoisie. The attitude of the masses toward Milyukov's party was one of the deepest hostility. At all elections during the revolutionary period, the Cadets suffered merciless defeat, and yet, the very parties — i.e., the Social-Revolutionists and Mensheviks — which victoriously defeated the Cadet party at the elections, after election gave it the place of honor in the coalition government. It is natural that the masses realized more and more that in reality the fusionist parties were playing the role of stewards to the liberal bourgeoisie.

Meantime, the internal situation was becoming more and more complicated and unfavorable. The war dragged on aimlessly, senselessly and interminably. The Government took no steps whatever to extricate itself from the vicious circle. The laughable scheme was proposed of sending the Menshevik Skobeloff to Paris to influence the allied imperialists. But no sane man attached any importance to this scheme. Korniloff gave up Riga to the Germans in order to terrorize public opinion, and having brought about this condition, to establish the discipline of the knout in the army. Danger threatened Petrograd. And the bourgeois elements greeted this peril with unconcealed malicious joy. The former President of the Duma, Rodzyanko, openly said again and again that the surrender of debauched Petrograd to the Germans would not be a great misfortune. For illustration he cited Riga, where the Deputy Soviets had been done away with after the coming of the Germans, and firm order, together with the old police system, had been established.

Would the Baltic fleet be lost? But the fleet had been debauched by the Revolutionary propaganda; ergo the loss was not so great. The cynicism of a garrulous nobleman expressed the hidden thoughts of the greater part of the bourgeoisie, that to surrender Petrograd to the Germans did not mean to lose it. Under the peace treaty it would be restored, but restored ravaged by German militarism. By that time the revolution would be decapitated, and it would be easier to manage. Kerensky's government did not think of seriously defending the capital. On the contrary, public opinion was being prepared for its possible surrender. Public institutions were being removed from Petrograd to Moscow and other cities.

In this setting, the Soldiers' section of the Petrograd Soviet had its meeting. Feeling was tense and turbulent, Was the Government incapable of defending Petrograd? If so, let it make peace. And if incapable of making peace, let it clear out. The frame of mind of the Soldiers' section found expression in this resolution. This was already the heat-lightning of the October Revolution.

At the front, the situation grew worse day by day. Chilly autumn, with its rains and winds, was drawing nigh. And there was looming up a fourth winter campaign. Supplies deteriorated every day. In the rear, the front had been forgotten — no reliefs, no new contingents, no warm winter clothing, which was indispensable. Desertions grew in number. The old army committees, elected in the first period of the Revolution, remained at their places and supported Kerensky's policy. Re-elections were forbidden. An abyss sprang up between the committees and the soldier masses. Finally the soldiers began to regard the committees with hatred. With increasing frequency delegates from the trenches were arriving in Petrograd and at the sessions of the Petrograd Soviet put the question point blank: "What is to be done further? By whom and how will the war be ended? Why is the Petrograd Soviet silent?"

Inevitability of the Struggle for Power

The Petrograd Soviet was not silent. It demanded the immediate transfer of all power into the hands of the Soviets in the capitals and in the provinces, the immediate transfer of the land to the peasants, the workingmen's control of production, and immediate opening of peace negotiations. So long as we remained an opposition party, the motto — all power to the Soviets — was a propaganda motto. But as soon as we found ourselves in the majority in all the principal Soviets, this motto imposed upon us the duty of a direct and immediate fight for power.

In the country villages, the situation had grown entangled and complicated in the extreme. The Revolution had promised land to the peasant, but at the same time, the leading parties demanded that the peasant should not touch this land until the Constituent Assembly should meet. At first the peasants waited patiently, but when they began to lose patience, the coalition ministry showered repressive measures upon them. Meanwhile the Constituent Assembly was receding to ever remoter distances. The bourgeoisie insisted upon calling the Constituent Assembly after the conclusion of peace. The peasant masses were growing more and more impatient. What we had foretold at the very beginning of the Revolution, was being realized: the peasants were seizing the land of their own accord. Repressive measures grew, arrests of revolutionary land committees began. In certain uyezds (districts) Kerensky introduced martial law. A line of delegates, who came on foot, flowed from the villages to the Petrograd Soviet. They complained that they had been arrested when they attempted to carry out the Petrograd Soviet's program and to transfer the estate holder's land into the hands of the peasant committees. The peasants demanded protection of us. We replied that we should be in a position to protect them only if the power were in our hands. From this, however, it followed that the Soviets must seize the power if they did not wish to become mere debating societies.

"It is senseless to fight for the power of the Soviets six or eight weeks before the Constituent Assembly," our neighbors on the Right told us. We, however, were in no degree infected with this fetish worship of the Constituent Assembly. In the first place, there were no guarantees that it really would be called. The breaking up of the army, mass desertions, disorganization of the supplies department, agrarian revolution – all this created an environment which was unfavorable to the elections for the Constituent Assembly. The surrender of Petrograd to the Germans, furthermore, threatened to remove altogether the question of elections from the order of the day. And, besides, even if it were called according to the old registration lists under the leadership of the old parties, the Constituent Assembly would be but a cover and a sanction for the coalition power. Without the bourgeoisie neither the S.R.'s nor the Mensheviks were in a position to assume power. Only the revolutionary class was destined to break the vicious circle wherein the Revolution was revolving and going to pieces. The power had to be snatched from the hands of the elements which were directly or indirectly serving the bourgeoisie and making use of the state apparatus as a tool of obstruction against the revolutionary demands of the people.

All power to the Soviets! demanded our party. Translated into party language, this had meant, in the preceding period, the power of the S.R.'s and Mensheviks, as opposed to a coalition with the liberal bourgeoisie. Now, in October 1917, the same motto meant handing over all power to the revolutionary proletariat, at the head of which, at this period, stood the Bolshevik party. It was a question of the dictatorship of the working class, which was leading, or, more correctly, was capable of leading the many millions of the poorest peasantry. This was the historical significance of the October uprising.

Everything led the party to this path. Since the first days of the Revolution, we had been preaching the necessity and inevitability of the power passing to the Soviets. After a great internal struggle, the majority of the Soviets made this demand their own, having accepted our point of view. We were preparing the Second All-Russian Congress of Soviets at which we: expected our party's complete victory. Under Dan's leadership (the cautious Cheidze had departed for the Caucasus), the Central Executive Committee attempted to block in every way the calling of the Congress of the Soviets. After great exertions, supported by the Soviet fraction of the Democratic Assembly, we finally secured the setting of the date of the Congress for October 25th. This date was destined to become the greatest day in the history of Russia. As a preliminary, we called in Petrograd a Congress of Soviets of the Northern regions, including the Baltic fleet and Moscow. At this Congress, we had a solid majority, and obtained a certain support on the right in the persons of the left S.R. faction, besides laying important organizational premises for the October uprising.

The Conflict Regarding the Petrograd Garrison

*B*ut even earlier, previous to the Congress of Northern Soviets, there occurred an event which was destined to play a most important role in the subsequent political struggle. Early in October there came to a meeting of the Petrograd Executive Committee, the Soviet's representative in the staff of the Petrograd Military District and announced that Headquarters demanded that two-thirds of the Petrograd garrison should be sent to the front. For what purpose? To defend Petrograd. They were not to be sent to the front at once, but still it was necessary to make ready immediately. The Staff recommended that the Petrograd Soviet approve this plan. We were on our guard. At the end of August, also, five revolutionary regiments, complete or in parts, had been taken out of Petrograd. This had been done at the request of the then Supreme Commander Korniloff, who at that very time was preparing to hurl a Caucasian division against Petrograd, with the intention of once for all settling with the revolutionary capital. Thus we had already the experience of purely political transfer of regiments under the pretext of military operations. Anticipating events. I shall say, that from documents brought to light after the October Revolution it became clear beyond any doubt that the proposed removal of the Petrograd garrison actually had nothing to do with military purposes, but was forced upon Commander-in-Chief Dukhonin, against his will, by none else but Kerensky, who was striving to clear the capital of the most revolutionary soldiers, i.e., those most hostile to him. But at that time, early in October, our suspicions evoked at first a storm of patriotic indignation. The Staff people were pressing us, Kerensky was impatient, for the ground under his feet had grown too hot. We, on the other hand, delayed answering. Danger undoubtedly threatened Petrograd and the question of defending the capital loomed before us in all its terrible significance. But after the Korniloff experience, after Rodzyanko's words concerning the desirability of the German occupation, whence should we take the assurance that Petrograd would not be maliciously given up to the Germans in punishment for its seditious spirit? The Executive Committee refused to affix its seal blindly to the order to transfer two-thirds of the garrison. It was necessary to verify, we said, whether there really were military considerations back of this order, and therefore it was necessary to create an organization for this verification. Thus was born the idea of creating – by the side of the Soldiers' section of the Soviet, i.e., the garrison's political representation – a purely military organization, in the form of a Military Revolutionary Committee, which subsequently acquired enormous power and became the real tool of the October Revolution. Undoubtedly, even in those hours, when putting forth the idea of creating an organization in whose hands would be concentrated the threads for guiding the Petrograd garrison on the purely military side, we clearly realized that this very organization might become an irreplaceable revolutionary tool. At that time we were already openly heading for the uprising, and were preparing for it in an organized way.

As indicated above, the All-Russian Congress of Soviets was ret for October 25th. There could be no longer any doubt that the Congress would declare itself in favor of power being handed over to the Soviets. But such a resolution must forthwith be put into actuality, else it would turn into a worthless, Platonic demonstration. The logic of events, therefore, required us to set the uprising for October 25th. Exactly so the entire bourgeois press interpreted it. But in the first place, the fate of the Congress depended upon the Petrograd garrison: would it allow Kerensky to surround the Congress of Soviets and disperse it with the assistance of several hundred or thousand military cadets, ensigns and thugs? Did not the very attempt to remove the garrison mean that the Government was preparing to disperse the Congress of Soviets? And strange it would be if it were not preparing, since we were, before the entire land, openly mobilizing the Soviet forces in order to deal the coalition forces a death blow.

Thus the conflict at Petrograd was developing on the basis of the question of the garrison's fate. First and foremost this question touched all the soldiers to the quick. But the working-men, too, felt the liveliest interest in the conflict, fearing as they did that upon the garrison's removal they would be smothered by the cadets and Cossacks. Thus the conflict was assuming a character of the very keenest nature and developing on a soil extremely unfavorable for Kerensky's government.

Parallel with this was going on the above-described struggle for convoking the All-Russian Congress of Soviets – we, openly declaring, in the name of the Petrograd Soviet and the Northern Region Congress, that the Second Congress of Soviets must set Kerensky's government aside and become the true master of the Russian land. As a matter of fact the uprising was already on. It was developing quite openly before the eyes of the whole country.

During October the question of the uprising played an important role in our party's inner life. Lenin, who was in hiding in Finland, insisted, in numerous letters, upon more resolute tactics. The lower strata were in ferment, and dissatisfaction was accumulating because the Bolshevik party, which had proved to be in the majority in the Petrograd Soviet, was drawing no practical conclusions from its own mottos. On October 10th a conspiratory meeting of the Central Committee of our party took place, with Lenin present. The question of the uprising was on the order of the day. By a majority of all against two votes it was decided that the only means of saving the Revolution and the country from final dissolution lay in armed insurrection which must transfer power into the hands of the Soviets.

The Democratic Soviet and "Pre-Parliament"

*T*he Democratic Soviet which had detached itself from the Democratic Conference had absorbed all the helplessness of the latter. The old Soviet parties, the Social-Revolutionists and the Mensheviks, had created an artificial majority in it for themselves, only the more strikingly to reveal their political prostration. Behind the Soviet curtains, Tseretelli was carrying on involved parleys with Kerensky and the representatives of the "professional elements" as they began to say in the Soviet, – in order to avoid the "insulting" term bourgeoisie.

Tseretelli's report on the course and issue of the negotiations was a sort of funeral oration over a whole period of the Revolution. It turned out that neither Kerensky nor the professional elements had consented to responsibility toward the new semi-representative institution. On the other hand, outside the limits of the Cadet Party, they had not succeeded in finding so-called "efficient" social leaders. The organizers of the venture had to capitulate on both points. The capitulation was all the more eloquent, because the Democratic Conference had been called exactly for the purpose of doing away with the irresponsible regime, while the Conference, by a formal vote, rejected a coalition with the Cadets. At several meetings of the Democratic Soviet which took place prior to the Revolution, there prevailed an atmosphere of tenseness and utter incapacity for action. The Soviet did not reflect the Revolution's march forward but the dissolution of the parties that had lagged behind the Revolution.

Even previous to the Democratic Conference, in our party faction, I had raised the question of demonstratively withdrawing from the Conference and boycotting the Democratic Soviet. It was necessary to show the masses by action that the fusionists had led the Revolution into a blind alley. The fight for building up the Soviet power could be carried on only in a revolutionary way. The power must be snatched from the hands of those who had proven incapable of doing any good and were furthermore even losing their capacity for active evil. Their method of working through an artificially picked Pre-Parliament and a conjectural Constituent Assembly, had to be opposed by our political method of mobilizing the forces around the Soviets, through the All-Russian Congress of Soviets and through insurrection. This could be done only by means of an open break, before the eyes of the entire people, with the body created by Tseretelli and his adherents, and by focusing on the Soviet institutions, the entire attention and all the forces of the working class. This is why I proposed the demonstrative withdrawal from the Conference and a revolutionary agitation, in shops and regiments, against the attempt to play false with the will of the Revolution and once again turn its progress into the channel of cooperation with the bourgeoisie. Lenin, whose letter we received a few days later, expressed himself to the same effect. But in the party's upper circles hesitation was still apparent on this question. The July days had left a deep impression in the party's consciousness. The mass of workingmen and soldiers had recovered from the July debacle much more rapidly than had many of the leading comrades who feared the nipping of the Revolution in the bud by a new premature onslaught of the masses. In our group of the Democratic Conference, I mustered 50 votes in favor of my proposal against 70 who declared for participating in the Democratic Council. However, the experience of this participation soon strengthened the party's left wing. It was growing too manifest that combinations bordering on trickery, combinations that aimed at securing further leadership in the Revolution for the professional elements, with the assistance of the fusionists, who had lost ground among the lower levels of the people, offered no escape from the impasse into which the laxness of bourgeois democracy had driven the revolution. By the time the Democratic Soviet, its ranks filled up with professional elements, became a Pre-Parliament, readiness to break with this institution had matured in our party.

The S.R.'s and Mensheviks

We were confronted with the question whether the S.R.'s would follow us in this path. This group was in the process of formation, but this process, according to the standards of our party, went on too slowly and irresolutely. At the outset of the Revolution, the S.R.'s proved the predominating party in the whole field of political life. Peasants, soldiers, even workingmen voted en masse for the S.R.'s. The party itself had not expected anything of the kind, and more than once it looked as if it were in danger of being swamped in the waves of its own success. Excluding the purely capitalistic and landholder groups and the professional elements among the intellectuals, one and all voted for the revolutionary populists' party. This was natural in the initial stage of the Revolution, when class lines had not had time to reveal themselves, when the aspirations of the so-called united revolutionary front found expression in the diffuse program of a party that was ready to welcome equally the workingman who feared to break away from the peasant; the peasant who was seeking land and liberty; the intellectual attempting to guide both of them; the chinovnik (officeholder) endeavoring to adjust himself to the new regime.

When Kerensky, who had been counted a laborite in the period of Czarism, joined the S.R.'s Party after the victory of the Revolution, that party's popularity began to grow in proportion as Kerensky mounted the rungs of power. Out of respect, not always of a platonic nature, for the War Minister, many colonels and generals hastened to enroll in the party of the erstwhile terrorists. Old S.R.'s, with revolutionary traditions, regarded with some uneasiness the ever increasing number of "March S.R.'s" that is, such party members as had discovered within themselves a revolutionary populist soul only in March, after the Revolution had overthrown the old regime and placed the revolutionary populists in authority. Thus, within the limits of its formlessness, this party contained not only the inner contradictions of the developing Revolution, but also the prejudices inherent in the backwardness of the peasant masses, and the sentimentalism, instability and career-chasing of the intellectual strata. It was perfectly clear that in that form the party could not last long. With regard to ideas, it proved impotent from the very start.

Politically, the guiding role belonged to the Mensheviks who had gone through the school of Marxism and derived from it certain procedures and habits, which aided them in finding their bearings in the political situation to the extent of scientifically falsifying the meaning of the current class struggle and securing the hegemony of the liberal bourgeoisie in the highest degree possible under the given circumstances. This is why the Mensheviks, direct pleaders for the bourgeoisie's right to power, exhausted themselves so rapidly and, by the time of the October Revolution, were almost completely played out.

The S.R.'s, too, were losing influence more and more — first among the workingmen, then in the army, and finally in the villages. But toward the time of the October upheaval, they remained still a very powerful party, numerically. However, class contradictions were undermining them from within. In opposition to the right wing which, in its most chauvinistic elements, such as Avksentyef, Breshko-Breshkovskaya, Savinkoff, etc., had finally gone over into the counter-revolutionary camp, a left wing was forming, which strove to preserve its connection with the toiling masses. If we merely recall the fact that the S.R., Avksentyef, as Minister of the Interior, arrested the Peasant Land Committees, composed of S.R.'s, for their arbitrary solution of the agrarian question, the amplitude of "differences" within this party will become sufficiently clear to us.

In its center stood the party's traditional leader, Chernoff. A writer of experience, well-read in socialist literature, an experienced hand in factional strife, he had constantly remained at the head of the party, when party life was being built up in emigrant circles abroad. The Revolution which had raised the S.R. party to an enormous height with its first indiscriminating wave, automatically raised Chernoff, too, only to reveal his complete impotence even as compared with the other leading political lights of the first period. The paltry resources which had secured to Chernoff a preponderance in the populist circles abroad, proved too light in the scales of the Revolution. He concentrated his efforts on not taking any responsible decisions, evading in all critical cases, waiting and abstaining. For some little time, tactics of this kind secured for him the position as center between the ever more diverging flanks. But there was no longer any possibility of preserving party unity for long. The former terrorist, Savinkof, took part in Korniloff's conspiracy, was in touching unanimity with the counter-revolutionary circles of Cossack officers and was preparing an onslaught on Petrograd workingmen and soldiers, among whom there were quite a few left S.R.'s. As a sacrifice to the left wing, the Center expelled Savinkof from the party, but hesitated to raise a hand against Kerensky. In the Pre-Parliament, the party showed signs of extreme disruption: three groups existed independently, though under the banner of one and the same party, but none of the groups knew exactly what it wanted. The formal domination of this "party" in the Constituent Assembly would have meant only a continuation of political prostration.

Withdrawing from the Pre-Parliament. The Voice of the Front

*B*efore withdrawing from the membership in the Pre-Parliament where, according to Kerensky's and Tseretelli's political statistics, we were entitled to some half a hundred seats, we arranged a conference with the left S.R. group. They refused to follow us, claiming that they still had to demonstrate practically before the peasantry the insolvency of the Pre-Parliament. Said one of the leaders of the left S.R.'s:

"We deem it necessary to warn you that if you want to withdraw from the Pre-Parliament in order forthwith to go into the streets for an open fight, we shall not follow you."

The bourgeois-fusionist press accused us of striving to kill prematurely the Pre-Parliament, for the very purpose of creating a revolutionary situation. At our faction meeting in the Pre-Parliament, it was decided to act independently and not wait for the left S.R.'s. Our party's declaration, proclaimed from the Pre-Parliament rostrum and explaining why we were breaking with this institution, was greeted with a howl of hatred and impotence on the part of the majority groups. In the Petrograd Soviet of Deputies, where our withdrawal from the Pre-Parliament was approved by an overwhelming majority, the leader of the tiny "internationalist" Menshevik group, Martof, explained to us that the withdrawal from the temporary Soviet of the Republic (such was the official appellation of this little-respected institution) would be sensible only in case we proposed immediately to assume an open offensive. But the point is that this is just what we intended. The prosecutors for the liberal bourgeoisie were right, when accusing us of striving to create a revolutionary situation. In open insurrection and direct seizure of power we beheld the only way out of the situation.

Again, as in the July days, the press and all the other organs of
so-called public opinion were mobilized against us. From the July
arsenals were dragged forth the most envenomed weapons which had
been temporarily stored away there after the Korniloff days. Vain efforts!
The mass was irresistibly moving toward us, and its spirit was rising
hour by hour. From the trenches delegates kept arriving. "How long,"
said they, at the Petrograd Soviet meetings, "will this impossible situation last? The soldiers have told us to declare to you: if no decisive
steps for peace are made by November 1st, the trenches will be deserted,
the entire army will rush to the rear!" This determination was really
spreading at the front. There the soldiers were passing on, from one unit
to another, home-made proclamations, summoning them not to remain
in the trenches later than the first snowfall. "You have forgotten about
us," the delegates on foot from the trenches exclaimed at the Soviet
meetings. "If you find no way out of the situation, we shall come here
ourselves, and with our bayonets we shall disperse our enemies, including you." In the course of a few weeks the Petrograd Council had become
the center of attraction for the whole army. After its leading tendency
had been changed and new presiding officers elected, its resolutions
inspired the exhausted and despondent troops at the front with the hope
that the way out of the situation could be practically found in the
manner proposed by the Bolsheviks: by publishing the secret treaties
and proposing an immediate truce on all fronts. "You say that power
must pass into the hands of the Soviets, grasp it then. Yon fear that the
front will not support you. Cast all misgivings aside, the soldier masses
are with you in overwhelming majority."

Meanwhile the conflict regarding the transfer of the garrison kept on
developing. Almost daily, a garrison conference met, consisting of
committees from the companies, regiments and commands. The influence of our party in the garrison was established definitely and inde-
structibly. The Petrograd District Staff was in a state of extreme perplexity. Now it would attempt to enter into regular relations with us, then
again, egged on by the leaders of the Central Executive Committee, it
would threaten us with repressive measures.

Above, mention has already been made of organizing, at the Petrograd Soviet, a Military Revolutionary Committee, which was intended
to be, in fact, the Soviet Staff of the Petrograd garrison in opposition
to Kerensky's Staff. "But the existence of two staffs is inadmissible," the
representatives of the fusionist parties dogmatically admonished us.
"But is a situation admissible, wherein the garrison mistrusts the official
staff and fears that the transfer of soldiers from Petrograd has been
dictated by a new counter-revolutionary machination?" we retorted.

"The creation of a second staff means insurrection," came the reply from the Right. "Your Military Revolutionary Committee's task will not be so much to verify the operative projects and orders of the military authorities as the preparation and execution of an insurrection against the present government." This objection was just: But for that very reason it did not frighten anybody. An overwhelming majority of the Soviet was aware of the necessity of overthrowing the coalition power. The more circumstantially the Mensheviks and S.R.'s demonstrated that the Military Revolutionary Committee would inevitably turn into an organ of insurrection, the greater the eagerness with which the Petrograd Soviet supported the new fighting organization.

The Military Revolutionary Committee's first act was to appoint commissioners to all parts of the Petrograd garrison and all the most important institutions of the capital and environs. From various quarters we were receiving communications that the government, or more correctly, the government parties, were actively organizing and arming their forces. From various arms-depots-governmental and private-rifles, revolvers, machine guns and cartridges were being brought forth for arming cadets, students and bourgeois youths in general. It was necessary to take immediate preventive measures. Commissioners were appointed to all arms-depots and stores. Almost without opposition they became masters of the situation. To be sure, the commandants and proprietors of the depots tried not to recognize them, but a mere application to the soldiers' committee or the employees of each institution sufficed to cause the immediate breakdown of the opposition. After that, arms were issued only on order of our Commissioners.

Even prior to that, regiments of the Petrograd garrison had their commissioners, but these had been appointed by the Central Executive Committee. Above, we said that after the June Congress of Soviets, and particularly after the June 18th demonstration which revealed the ever growing power of the Bolsheviks, the fusionist parties had almost entirely deprived the Petrograd Soviet of any practical influence on the course of events in the revolutionary capital. The leadership of the Petrograd garrison was concentrated in the hands of the Central Executive Committee. Now the task everywhere was to put in the Petrograd Soviet's Commissioners. This was achieved with the most energetic cooperation of the soldier masses. Meetings, addressed by speakers of various parties, had the result, invariably, that regiment after regiment declared it would recognize only the Petrograd Soviet's Commissioners and would not budge a step without its decision.

An important role in appointing these Commissioners was played by the Bolsheviks' military organization. Before the July days it had developed a widespread agitational activity. On July 5th, a battalion of cyclists, brought by Kerensky to Petrograd, battered down the isolated Kshessinsky mansion where our party's military organization was quartered. The majority of leaders, and many privates among the members were arrested, the publications were stopped, the printing shop was wrecked. Only by degrees did the organization begin to repair its machinery afresh, conspiratively this time. Numerically it comprised in its ranks but a very insignificant part of the Petrograd garrison, a few hundred men all told. But there were among them many soldiers and young officers, chiefly ensigns, resolute, and with heart and soul devoted to the Revolution, who had passed through Kerensky's prisons in July and August. All of them had placed themselves at the Military Revolutionary Committee's disposal and were being assigned to the most responsible fighting posts.

However, it would not be superfluous to remark that precisely the members of our party's military organization assumed in October an attitude of extraordinary caution and even some skepticism toward the idea of an immediate insurrection. The closed character of the organization and its officially military character involuntarily inclined its leaders to underestimate the purely technical and organizational resources of the uprising, and from this point of view we were undoubtedly weak. Our strength lay in the revolutionary enthusiasm of the masses and their readiness to fight under our banner.

Parallel with the organizing activity a stormy agitation was being carried on. This was the period of incessant meetings at works, in the "Modern" and "Chinizelli" circuses, at clubs, in barracks. The atmosphere at all the meetings was charged with electricity. Each mention of the insurrection was greeted with a storm of plaudits and shouts of delight. The bourgeois press merely increased the state of universal panic. An order issued over my signature to the Syestroyetsk munitions factory to issue five thousand rifles to the Red Guard evoked an indescribable panic in bourgeois circles. "The general massacre" in course of preparation was talked and written about everywhere. Of course, this did not in the least prevent the workingmen of the Syestroyetsk munitions factory from handing the arms over to the Red Guards. The more frantically the bourgeois press slandered and baited us, the more ardently the masses responded to our call. It was growing clearer and clearer for both sides that the crisis must break within the next few days. The press of the S.R.'s and Mensheviks was sounding an alarm. "The Revolution is in the greatest danger. A repetition of the July days is being prepared — but on a much wider basis and therefore still more destructive in its consequences." In his Novaya Zhizn, Gorki daily prophesied the approaching wreck of all civilization. In general, the Socialistic veneer of the bourgeois intellectuals was wearing off at the approach of the stern domination of the workers' dictatorship. But, on the other hand, the soldiers of even the most backward regiments hailed with delight the Military Revolutionary Committee's commissioners. Delegates came to us from Cossack units and from the Socialist minority of military cadets. They promised at least to assure the neutrality of their units in case of open conflict. Manifestly Kerensky's government was losing its foundations.

The District Staff began negotiations with us and proposed a compromise. In order to size up the enemy's full resistance, we entered into pourparlers. But the Staff was nervous; now they exhorted, then threatened us, they even declared our commissioners to be without power, which, however, did not in the least affect their work. In accord with the Staff, the Central Executive Committee appointed Captain of Staff Malefski to be Chief Commissioner for the Petrograd Military District and magnanimously consented to recognize our commissioners, on condition of their being subordinate to the Chief Commissioner. The proposal was rejected and the negotiations broken off. Prominent Mensheviks and S.R.'s came to us as intermediaries, exhorted, threatened and foretold our doom and the doom of the Revolution.

The "Petrograd Soviet Day"

At this period the Smolny building was already completely in the hands of the Petrograd Soviet and of our party. The Mensheviks and the S.R.'s transferred their political activity to the Maryiinsky Palace, where the infant Pre-Parliament was already expiring. In the Pre-Parliament Kerensky delivered a great speech, in which, stormily applauded by the bourgeois wing, he endeavored to conceal his impotence behind clamorous threats. The Staff made its last attempt at opposition. To all units of the garrison it sent out invitations to appoint two delegates to conferences concerning the removal of troops from the capital. The first conference was called for October 22nd, at 11 p.m. From the regiments we immediately received information about it. By telephone we issued a call for a garrison conference at 11 a.m. Withal, a part of the delegates did get to the Staff quarters, only to declare that without the Petrograd Soviet's decision they would not move anywhere. Almost unanimously the Garrison Conference confirmed its allegiance to the Military Revolutionary Committee. Objections came only from official representatives of the former Soviet parties, but they found no response whatever among the regimental delegates. The Staff's attempt brought out only more strikingly that we were standing on firm ground. In the front rank there was the Volhynian Regiment, the very one which on July 4th, with its band playing, had invaded the Tauri'da Palace, in order to put down the Bolsheviks.

As already mentioned earlier, the Central Executive Committee had charge of the Petrograd Soviet's treasury and its publications. An attempt to obtain even a single one of these publications brought no results. Beginning with the end of September, we initiated a series of measures toward creating an independent newspaper of the Petrograd Soviet. But all printing establishments were occupied and their owners boycotted us with the assistance of the Central Executive Committee. It was decided to arrange for a "Petrograd Soviet Day," for the purpose of developing a widespread agitation and collecting pecuniary resources for establishing a newspaper. About a fortnight before, this day was set for October 22nd, and consequently it coincided with the moment of the open outburst of the insurrection.

With complete assurance, the hostile press announced that on October 22nd an armed insurrection of the Bolsheviks would occur in the streets of Petrograd. That the insurrection would occur, nobody had any doubt. They only tried to determine exactly when; they guessed, they prophesied, striving in this way to force a denial or confession on our part. But the Soviet calmly and confidently marched forward, making no answer to the howl of bourgeois public opinion. October 22nd became the reviewing day for the forces of the proletarian army. It went off magnificently in every respect. In spite of the warnings coming from the Right that blood would flow in torrents in the streets of Petrograd, the masses of the populace were pouring in floods to the Petrograd Soviet meetings. All our oratorical forces were mobilized. All public places were filled. Meetings were held unceasingly for hours at a stretch. They were addressed by speakers of our party, by delegates arriving for the Soviet Congress, by representatives from the front, by left S.R.'s and by Anarchists. Public buildings were flooded by waves of working-men, soldiers and sailors. There had not been many gatherings like that even in the time of the Revolution. Up rose a considerable mass of the petty townfolk, less frightened than aroused by the shouts, warnings and baiting of the bourgeois press. Waves of people by tens of thousands dashed against the People's House building, rolled through the corridors, filled the halls. On the iron columns huge garlands of human heads, feet and hands were hanging like bunches of grapes. The air was surcharged with the electric tension that heralds the most critical moments of revolution. "Down with Kerensky's government! Down with the war! All power to the Soviets!" Not one from the ranks of the previous Soviet parties ventured to appear before those colossal throngs with a word of reply. The Petrograd Soviet held undivided sway. In reality the campaign had already been won. It only remained to deal the last military blow to this spectral authority.

The most cautious in our midst were reporting that there still remained units that were not with us: the Cossacks, the cavalry regiment, the Semyonofski regiment, the cyclists. Commissioners and agitators were assigned to these units. Their reports sounded perfectly satisfactory: the red-hot atmosphere was infecting one and all, and the most conservative elements of the army were losing the strength to withstand the general tendency of the Petrograd garrison. In the Semyonofski regiment, which was considered the bulwark of Kerensky's government, I was present at a meeting which took place in the open air. The most prominent speakers of the right wing addressed it. They clung to the conservative guard regiments as to the last support of the coalition power. Nothing would avail. By an overwhelming majority of votes, the regiment expressed itself for us and did not even give the ex-ministers a chance to finish their speeches. The groups which still opposed the Soviet watch-words were made up mainly of officers, volunteers and generally of bourgeois intellectuals and semi-intellectuals. The masses of peasants and workmen were with us one and all. The demarcation ran as a distinct social line.

The Fortress of Peter and Paul is the central military base of Petrograd. As commandant thereof we appointed a young ensign. He proved the best man for the post and within a few hours he became master of the situation. The lawful authorities withdrew, biding their time. The element regarded as unreliable for us were the cyclists, who in July had smashed our party's military organization in the Kshessinsky mansion and taken possession of the mansion itself. On the 23rd, I went to the Fortress about 2 p.m. Within the courtyard a meeting was being held. The speakers of the right wing were cautious and evasive in the extreme, painstakingly avoiding the question of Kerensky, whose name inevitably aroused shouts of protest and indignation even among the soldiers. We were listened to, and our advice vas followed. About four o'clock, the cyclists assembled nearby, in the "Modern" Circus, for a battalion meeting. Among the speakers appearing there was Quartermaster-General Paradyelof. He spoke with extreme caution. The days had been left far behind, when official and semi-official speakers referred to the party of the workers merely as to a gang of traitors and hired agents of the German Kaiser.

The Lieutenant-Commander of the Staff accosted me with: "We really ought to be able to come to some agreement." But it was already too late. The whole battalion, with only thirty dissenting votes, had voted for handing over all power to the Soviets.

The Beginning of the Revolution

The government of Kerensky was restlessly looking for refuge, now one way, now another. Two new cyclist battalions, and the Zenith Battery were called back from the front, and an attempt was made to call back some companies of cavalry. . . . The cyclists telegraphed while on the road to the Petrograd Soviet: "We are led to Petrograd without knowing the reasons. Request explanations." We ordered them to stop and send a delegation to Petrograd. Their representatives arrived and declared at a meeting of the Soviet that the battalion was entirely with us. This was greeted by enthusiastic cheers. The battalion received orders to enter the city immediately.

The number of delegates from the front was increasing every day. They came to get information about the situation. They gathered our literature and went to bring the message to the front that the Petrograd Soviet was conducting a struggle for the power of the workers, soldiers and peasants. "The men in the trenches will support you," they told us. All the old army committees which had not been reelected for the last four or five months, sent threatening telegrams to us, which, however, made no impression. We knew that these committees were no less out of touch with the rank and file of the soldiers than the Central Executive Committee with the local Soviets.

The Military Revolutionary Committee appointed commissaries to all railroad depots. These commissaries kept a watchful eye upon all the arriving and departing trains and especially upon the movements of troops. Continuous telephone and motorcar communication was established with the neighboring cities and their garrisons. The Soviets of all the communities near Petrograd were charged with the duty of vigilantly preventing any counter-revolutionary troops, or, rather, troops misled by the government, from entering the capital. The railroad officials of lower rank and the workmen recognized our commissaries immediately. Difficulties arose on the 24th at the telephone station. They stopped connecting us. The cadets took possession of the station and under their protection the telephone operators began to oppose the Soviet. This was the first appearance of the future sabotage. The Military Revolutionary Committee sent a detachment to the telephone station and placed two small cannons there. In this way the seizing of all departments of the government and instruments of administration was started. The sailors and Red Guards occupied the telegraph station, the post office and other institutions. Measures were taken to take possession of the state bank. The center of the government, the Institute of Smolny, was turned into a fortress. There were in the garret, as a heritage of the old Central Executive Committee, a score of machine guns, but they were in poor condition and had been entirely neglected by the caretakers. We ordered an additional machine gun company to the Smolny Institute. Early in the morning the sailors rolled the machine gun with a deafening rumble over the cement floors of the long and half-dark corridors of the building. Out of the doors the frightened faces of the few S.R.'s and Mensheviks were looking and wondering.

The Soviet held daily meetings in the Smolny and so did the Garrison Council.

On the third floor of the Smolny, in a small corner room, the Military Revolutionary Committee was in continuous session. There was centered all the information about the movements of the troops, the spirit of the soldiers and workers, the agitation in the barracks, the undertakings of the pogrom instigators, the councils of the bourgeois politicians, the life at the Winter Palace, the plans of the former Soviet parties. Informers came from all sides. There came workers, officers, porters, Socialist cadets, servants, ladies. Many brought pure nonsense. Others gave serious and valuable information. The decisive moment drew near. It was apparent that there was no going back.

On the evening of the 24th of October, Kerensky appeared in the Preliminary Parliament and demanded approval of repressive measures against the Bolsheviki. The Preliminary Parliament, however, was in a sad state of indetermination and complete disintegration. The Constitutional Democrats tried to persuade the right S.R.'s to adopt a vote of confidence. The right S.R.'s exercised pressure upon the center. The center hesitated. The "left" wing conducted a policy of parliamentary opposition. After many conferences, debates, hesitations, the resolution of the "left" wing was adopted. This resolution condemned the rebellious movement of the Soviet, but the responsibilities for the movement were laid at the door of the anti-democratic policy of the government. The mail brought scores of letters daily informing us of death sentences pronounced against us, of infernal machines, of the expected blowing up of the Smolny, etc. The bourgeois press howled wildly, moved by hatred and terror. Gorki, who had forgotten all about "The Song of the Falcon," continued to prophesy in his Novaya Zhizn the approach of the end of the world.

The members of the Military Revolutionary Committee did not leave the Smolny during the entire week. They slept on sofas and only at odd intervals, wakened by couriers, scouts, cyclists, telegraph messengers and telephone calls. The night of the 24th-25th was the most restless. We received a telephone communication from Pavlovsky that the government had called artillery from the Peterhof School of Ensigns. At the Winter Palace, Kerensky gathered the cadets and officers. We gave out orders over the telephone to place on all the roads leading to Petrograd reliable military defense and to send agitators to meet the military detachment called by the government. In case persuasion would not help they were instructed to use armed force. All the negotiations were held over the telephone in the open, and therefore were accessible to the agents of the government.

The commissaries informed us over the telephone that on all the roads leading to Petrograd our friends were on the alert. A cadet detachment from Oranienbaum nevertheless succeeded in getting by our military defense during the night and over the telephone we followed their further movements. The outer guard of the Smolny was strengthened by another company. Communications with all the detachments of the garrison went on continuously.

The companies on guard in all the regiments were awake. The delegates of every detachment were day and night at the disposal of the Military Revolutionary Committee. An order was given to suppress the agitation of the Black Hundred without reserve, and at the first attempts at pogroms on the streets, arms should be used without mercy.

During this decisive night all the most important points of the city passed into our hands — almost without any opposition, without struggle and without bloodshed. The State Bank was guarded by a government detachment and an armored car. The building was surrounded on all sides by our troops. The armored car was taken by an unexpected attack and the bank went over into the hands of the Military Revolutionary Committee without a single shot being fired. There was on the river Neva, behind the Franco-Russian plant, the cruiser Aurora, which was under repair. Its crew consisted entirely of sailors devotedly loyal to the revolution. When Korniloff, at the end of August, threatened Petrograd the sailors of the Aurora were called by the government to guard the Winter Palace, and though even then they already hated the government of Kerensky, they realized that it was their duty to dam the wave of the counter-revolution, and they took their post without objection. When the danger passed they were sent back. Now, in the days of the October uprising, they were too dangerous. The Aurora was ordered by the Minister of the Navy to weigh anchor and to get out of Petrograd. The crew informed us immediately of this order. We annulled it and the cruiser remained where it was, ready at any moment to put all its military forces and means at the disposal of the Soviets.

The Decisive Day

At the dawn of the 25th, a man and woman, employed in the party's printing office, came to Smolny and informed us that the government had closed the official journal of our body and the "New Gazette" of the Petrograd Soviet. The printing office was sealed by some agent of the government. The Military Revolutionary Committee immediately recalled the orders and took both publications under its protection, enjoining upon the "gallant Wolinsky Regiment the great honor of securing the free Socialist press against counter-revolutionary attempts." The printing, after that, went on without interruption and both publications appeared on time.

The government was still in session at the Winter Palace, but it was no more than its own shadow. As a political power it no longer existed. On the 25th of October the Winter Palace was gradually surrounded by our troops from all sides. At one o'clock in the afternoon I declared at the session of the Petrograd Soviet, in the name of the Military Revolutionary Committee, that the government of Kerensky had ceased to exist and that forthwith, and until the All-Russian Convention of the Soviets might decide otherwise, the power was to pass into the hands of the Military Revolutionary Committee.

A few days earlier Lenin left Finland and was hiding in the outskirts of the city, in the workingmen's quarters. On the evening of the 25th, he came secretly to the Smolny. According to newspaper information, it seemed to him that the issue would be a temporary compromise between ourselves and the Kerensky Government. The bourgeois press had so often clamored about the approach of the revolution, about the demonstration of armed soldiers on the streets, about pillaging and unavoidable streams of blood, that now this press failed to notice the revolution which was really taking place, and accepted the negotiations of the general staff with us at their face value. Meanwhile, without any chaos, without street fights, without firing or bloodshed, the government institutions were occupied one after another by severe and disciplined detachments of soldiers, sailors and Red Guards, in accordance with the exact telephone orders given from the small room on the third floor of the Smolny Institute. In the evening a preliminary session of the Second All-Russian Convention of Soviets was held. In the name of the Central Executive Committee, Dan presented a report. He presented an indictment of the rebellious usurpers and insurgents and attempted to frighten the Convention with a vision of the inevitable failure of the insurrection, which, he claimed, would be suppressed by the forces from the front. His address sounded unconvincing and out of place within the walls of a hall where the overwhelming majority of the delegates were enthusiastically observing the victorious advance of the Petrograd revolution.

By this time the Winter Palace was surrounded, but it was not yet taken. From time to time there were shots from the windows upon the besiegers, who were closing in slowly and cautiously. From the Petropavlovsk Fortress, two or three shells from cannons were directed at the Palace. Their thunder was heard at the Smolny. Martof spoke with helpless indignation from the platform of the convention, about civil war and especially about the siege of the Winter Palace, where among the ministers there were − oh, horror! − members of the Mensheviki party. The sailors who came to bring information from the battle-place around the Palace took the floor against him. They reminded the accusers of the offensive of the 18th of June, of the treacherous policy of the old government, of the re-establishment of the death penalty for soldiers, of the annihilation of the revolutionary organization, and wound up by vowing to win or die. They also brought word of the first victims from our ranks in the battle before the Palace.

All arose as if at an unseen signal and, with a unanimity which could be created only by a high moral inspiration, sang the Funeral March. He who lived through that moment will never forget it.

The session was interrupted. It was impossible to deliberate theoretically the question of the means of reconstructing the government among the echoes of the fighting and shooting under the walls of the Winter Palace, where the fate of that very government was being decided in a practical way. The taking of the Palace, however, was rather slow, and this caused hesitation among the less determined elements of the convention. The orators of the right wing prophesied our near destruction. All anxiously awaited news from the arena of the Palace. Presently Antonoff appeared, who directed the operations against the Palace. A deathlike silence fell upon the hall. The Winter Palace was taken; Kerensky had fled; other ministers had been arrested and consigned to the fortress of Petropavlovsk. The first chapter of the October revolution was over.

The Right Revolutionists and the Mensheviki, altogether sixty men, that is, about one-tenth of the convention, left the session in protest. As there was nothing else left to' them, they "placed the entire responsibility" for the coming events upon the Bolsheviki and Left S.R.'s. The latter were passing through moments of indecision. The past tied them strongly to the party of Chernoff. The right wing of this party swerved to the middle and petty bourgeois elements, to the intellectuals of the middle classes, to the well-to-do elements of the villages; and on all decisive questions went hand in hand with the liberal bourgeoisie against us. The more revolutionary elements of the party, reflecting the radicalism of the social demands of the poorest masses of the peasantry, gravitated to the proletariat and their party. They feared, however, to sever the umbilical cord which linked them to their old party. When we left the Preliminary Parliament, they refused to follow us and warned us against "adventurers," but the insurrection put before them the dilemma of taking sides for or against the Soviets. Not without hesitation, they assembled on our side of the barricades.

The Formation of the Soviet of the People's Commissaries

*T*he victory in Petrograd was complete. The power went over entirely to the Military Revolutionary Committee. We issued our first decree, abolishing the death penalty and ordering reelections in the army committees, etc. But here we discovered that we were cut off from the provinces. The higher authorities of the railroads, post office and telegraph were against us. The army committees, the municipalities, the zemstvos continued to bombard the Smolny with threatening telegrams in which they declared outright war upon us and promised to sweep the insurgents out within a short time. Our telegrams, decrees and explanations did not reach the provinces, for the Petrograd Telegraph Agency refused to serve us. In this atmosphere, created by the isolation of the capital from the rest of the country, alarming and monstrous rumors easily sprang up and gained popularity.

When finally convinced that the Soviet had really taken over the powers of the government, that the old government was arrested, that the streets of Petrograd were dominated by armed workers, the bourgeois press, as well as the press which was for effecting a compromise, started a campaign of incomparable madness indeed; there was not a lie or libel which was not mobilized against the Military Revolutionary Committee, its leaders or its commissaries.

On the 26th there was a session of the Petrograd Soviet, which was attended by delegates from the All-Russian Council, members of the Garrison Conference, and numerous members of various parties. Here, for the first time in nearly six months, spoke Lenin and Zinoviev, who were given a stormy ovation. The jubilation over the recent victory was marred somewhat by apprehensions as to how the country would take to the new revolt and as to the Soviets' ability to retain control.

In the evening an executive session of the Council of Soviets was held. Lenin introduced two decrees: on peace and on the land question.

After brief discussion, both decrees were adopted unanimously. It was at this session, too, that a new central authority was created, to be known as the Council of People's Commissaries.

The Central Committee of our party tried to win the approval of the Left S.R.'s, who were invited to participate in establishing the Soviet government. They hesitated, on the ground that, in their view, this government should bear a coalition character within the Soviet parties. But the Mensheviki and the Right S.R.'s broke entirely with the Council of Soviets, deeming a coalition with anti-Soviet parties necessary. There was nothing left for us to do but to let the party of Left S.R.'s persuade their neighbors to the right to return to the revolutionary camp; and while they were engaged in this hopeless task, we thought it our duty to take the responsibility for the government entirely upon our party. The list of Peoples' Commissaries was composed exclusively of Bolsheviki.

There was undoubtedly some political danger in such a course. The change proved too precipitate. (One need but remember that the leaders of this party were only yesterday still under indictment under Statute Law No. 108 — that is, accused of high treason). But there was no other alternative. The other Soviet groups hesitated and evaded the issue, preferring to adopt a waiting policy. Finally we became convinced that only our party could set up a revolutionary government.

The First Days of the New Regime

The decrees on land and peace, approved by the Council, were printed in huge quantities and — through delegates from the front, peasant pedestrians arriving from the villages, and agitators sent by us to the trenches in the provinces — were strewn broadcast all over the country. Simultaneously the work of organizing and arming the Red Guards was carried on. Together with the old garrison and the sailors, the Red Guard was doing hard patrol duty. The Council of People's Commissaries got control of one government department after another, though everywhere encountering the passive resistance of the higher and middle grade officials. The former Soviet parties tried their utmost to find support in this class and organize a sabotage of the new government. Our enemies felt certain that the whole affair was a mere episode, that in a day or two — at most a week — the Soviet Government would be overthrown. The first foreign councilors and members of the embassies, impelled quite as much by curiosity as by necessary business on hand, appeared at the Smolny Institute. Newspaper correspondents hurried thither with their notebooks and cameras. Everyone hastened to catch a glimpse of the new government, being sure that in a day or two it would be too late.

Perfect order reigned in the city. The sailors, soldiers and the Red Guards bore themselves in these first days with excellent discipline and nobly supported the regime of stern revolutionary order.

In the enemy's camp fear arose lest the "episode" should become too protracted, and so the first force for attacking the new government was being hastily organized. In this, the initiative was taken by the Social-Revolutionists and the Mensheviki. In the preceding period they would not, and dared not, take all the power into their own hands. In keeping with their provisional political position, they contented themselves with serving in the coalition government in the capacity of assistants, critics, and benevolent accusers and defenders of the bourgeoisie. During all elections they conscientiously anathematized the liberal bourgeoisie, while in the government they just as regularly combined with it. In the first six months of the revolution they managed, as a result of this policy, to lose absolutely all the confidence of the populace and army; and now, the October revolt was dashing them from the helm of the state. And yet, only yesterday they considered themselves the masters of the situation. The Bolshevik leaders whom they persecuted were in hiding, as under Czarism. Today the Bolsheviki were in power, while yesterday's coalitionist ministers and their co-workers found themselves cast aside and suddenly deprived of every bit of influence upon the further course of events. They would not and could not believe that this sudden revolt marked the beginning of a new era. They preferred to consider it as merely accidental, the result of some misunderstanding, which could be removed by a few energetic speeches and accusational newspaper articles. But every hour they encountered more and more insurmountable obstacles. This is what caused their blind, truly furious hatred.

The bourgeois politicians did not venture, to be sure, to get too close to danger. They pushed to the front the Social-Revolutionists and Mensheviki, who, in the attack upon us acquired all that energy which they had lacked during the period when they were a semi-governing power. Their organs circulated the most amazing rumors and lies. In their name it was that the proclamations containing open appeals to crush the new government were issued. It was they, too, who organized the government officials for sabotage and the cadets for military resistance.

On the 27th and 28th we continued to receive persistent threats by telegraph from army committees, town dumas, vikzhel zemstvos, and organizations (which had charge of the management of the Railroad Union). On the Nevsky Prospect, the principal thoroughfare of the capital's bourgeoisie, things were becoming more and more lively. The bourgeois youth was emerging from its stupor and, urged on by the press, was developing a wider and wider agitation against the Soviet government. With the help of the bourgeois crowd, the cadets were disarming individual Red Guardsmen. On the side-streets Red Guardsmen and sailors were being shot down. A group of cadets seized the telephone station. Attempts were made by the same side to seize the telegraph office. Finally, we learned that three armored cars had fallen into the hands of some inimical military organization. The bourgeois elements were clearly raising their heads. The newspapers heralded the fact that we had but a few hours more to live. Our friends intercepted a few secret orders which made it clear, however, that a militant organization had been formed to fight the Petrograd Soviet. The leading place in this organization was taken by the so-called Committee for the Defense of the Revolution, organized by the local Duma and the Central Executive Committee of the former regime. Here and there Right Social-Revolutionists and Mensheviki held sway. At the disposal of this committee were the cadets, students, and many counter-revolutionary army officers, who sought, from under cover of the coalitions, to deal the Soviets a mortal blow.

The Cadet Uprising of October 29th

*T*he stronghold of the counter-revolutionary organization was the cadet schools and the Engineering Castle, where considerable arms and ammunition were stored, and from where attacks were made upon the revolutionary government's headquarters. Detachments of Red Guards and sailors had surrounded the cadet schools and were sending in messengers demanding the surrender of all arms. Some scattering shots came in reply. The besiegers were trampled upon. Crowds of people gathered around them, and not infrequently stray shots fired from the windows would wound passers-by.

The skirmishes were assuming an indefinitely prolonged character, and this threatened the revolutionary detachments with demoralization. It was necessary, therefore, to adopt the most determined measures. The task of disarming the cadets was assigned to the commandant of Petropavlovsk fortress, Ensign B. He closely surrounded the cadet schools, brought up some armored cars and artillery, and gave the cadets ten minutes' time to surrender. Renewed firing from the windows was the answer at first. At the expiration of the ten minutes, B. ordered an artillery charge. The very first shots made yawning breaches in the walls of the schoolhouse. The cadets surrendered, though many of them tried to save themselves by flight, firing as they fled.

Considerable rancor was created, such as always accompanies civil war. The sailors undoubtedly committed many outrages upon individual cadets. The bourgeois press later accused the sailors and the Soviet government of inhumanity and brutality. It never mentioned, however, the fact that the revolt of October 25th-26th had been brought about with hardly any firing or sacrifice, and that only the counter-revolutionary conspiracy which was organized by the bourgeoisie and which threw the young generation into the flame of civil war against the workers, soldiers and sailors, led to unavoidable severities and sacrifices.

The 29th of October marked a decided change in the mood of the inhabitants of Petrograd. Events took on a more tragic character. At the same time, our enemies realized that the situation was far more serious than they thought at first and that the Soviet had not the slightest intention of relinquishing the power it had won just to oblige the junkers and the capitalistic newspapers.

The work of clearing Petrograd of counter-revolutionary centers was carried on intensively. The cadets were almost all disarmed, the participators in the insurrection were arrested and either imprisoned in the Petropavlovsk fortress or deported to Kronstadt. All publications which openly preached revolt against Soviet authority were promptly suppressed. Orders were issued for the arrest of such of the leaders of the former Soviet parties whose names figured on the intercepted counter-revolutionary edicts. All military resistance in the capital was crushed absolutely.

Next came a long and exhausting struggle against the sabotage of the bureaucrats, technical workers, clerks, etc. These elements, which by their earning capacity belong largely to the downtrodden class of society, align themselves with the bourgeois class by the conditions of their life and by their general psychology. They had sincerely and faithfully served the government and its institutions when it was headed by Czarism. They continued to serve the government when the authority passed over into the hands of the bourgeois imperialists. They were inherited with all their knowledge and technical skill, by the coalition government in the next period of the revolution. But when the revolting workingmen, soldiers and peasants flung the parties of the exploiting classes away from the rudder of State and tried to take the management of affairs into their own hands, then the bureaucrats and clerks flew into a passion and absolutely refused to support the new government in any way. More and more extensive became this sabotage, which was organized mostly by Social-Revolutionists and Mensheviki, and which was supported by funds furnished by the banks and the Allied Embassies.

Kerensky's Advance on Petrograd

The stronger the Soviet government became in Petrograd, the more the bourgeois groups placed their hopes on military aid from without. The Petrograd Telegraph Agency, the railroad telegraph, and the radio-telegraph station of Tsarskoye-Selo brought from every side news of huge forces marching on Petrograd with the object of crushing the rebels there and establishing order. Kerensky was making flying trips to the front, and the bourgeois papers reported that he was leading innumerable forces against the Bolsheviki. We found ourselves cut off from the rest of the country, as the telegraphers refused to serve us. But the soldiers, who arrived by tens and hundreds on commissions from their respective regiments, invariably said to us: "Have no fears of the front; it is entirely on your side. You need but give the word, and we will send to your aid — even this very day — a division or a corps." It was the same in the army as everywhere else; the masses were for us, and the upper classes against us. In the hands of the latter was the military-technical machinery. Various parts of the vast army proved to be isolated one from another. We were isolated from both the army and the people. Nevertheless, the news of the Soviet government at Petrograd and its decrees spread throughout the country and roused the local Soviets to rebel against the old government.

The reports of Kerensky's advance on Petrograd, at the head of some forces or other, soon became more persistent and assumed more definite outlines. We were informed from Tsarskoye-Selo that Cossack echelons were not far from there, while an appeal, signed by Kerensky and General Krassnov, was being circulated in Petrograd calling upon the whole garrison to join the government's forces, which were expected any hour to enter the capital. The cadet insurrection of October 29th was undoubtedly connected with Kerensky's undertaking, only that it broke out too soon, owing to determined action on our part. The Tsarskoye-Selo garrison was ordered to demand of the approaching Cossack regiments recognition of the Soviet government. In case of refusal, the

Cossacks were to be disarmed. But that garrison proved to be ill-fitted for military operations. It had no artillery and no leaders, its officers being unfriendly toward the Soviet government. The Cossacks took possession of the radio-telegraph station at Tsarskoye-Selo, the most powerful one in the country, and marched on. The garrisons of Peterhof, Krasnoye-Selo and Gatchina displayed neither initiative nor resolution.

After the almost bloodless victory at Petrograd, the soldiers confidently assumed that matters would take a similar course in the future. All that was necessary, they thought, was to send an agitator to the Cossacks, who would lay down their arms the moment the object of the proletarian revolution was explained to them. Korniloff's counter-revolutionary uprising was put down by means of speeches and fraternization. By agitation and well-planned seizure of certain institutions — without a fight — the Kerensky government was overthrown. The same methods were now being employed by the leaders of the Tsarskoye-Selo, Krasnoye-Selo and the Gatchina Soviets with General Krassnov's Cossacks. But this time they did not work. Though without determination or enthusiasm, the Cossacks did advance. Individual detachments approached Gatchina and Krasnoye-Selo, engaged the scanty forces of the local garrisons, and sometimes disarmed them. About the numerical strength of Kerensky's forces we at first had no idea whatever. Some said that General Krassnov headed ten thousand men; others affirmed that he had no more than a thousand; while the unfriendly newspapers and circulars announced, in letters an inch big, that two corps were lined up beyond Tsarskoye-Selo.

There was a general want of confidence in the Petrograd garrison. No sooner had it won a bloodless victory, than it was called upon to march out against an enemy of unknown numbers and engage in battles of uncertain outcome. In the Garrison Conference, the discussion centered about the necessity of sending out more and more agitators and of issuing appeals to the Cossacks; for to the soldiers it seemed impossible that the Cossacks would refuse to rise to the point of view which the Petrograd garrison was defending in its struggle. Nevertheless, advanced groups of Cossacks approached quite close to Petrograd, and we anticipated that the principal battle would take place in the streets of the city.

The greatest resolution was shown by the Red Guards. They demanded arms, ammunition, and leadership. But everything in the military machine was disorganized and out of gear, owing partly to disuse and partly to evil intent. The officers had resigned. Many had fled. The rifles were in one place and the cartridges in another. Matters were still worse with artillery. The cannons, gun carriages and the military stores were all in different places; and all these had to be groped for in the dark. The various regiments did not have at their disposal either sappers' tools or field telephones. The Revolutionary General Staff, which tried to straighten out things from above, encountered insurmountable obstacles, the greatest of which was the sabotage of the military-technical employees.

Then we decided to appeal directly to the working class. We stated that the success of the revolution was most seriously threatened, and that it was for them — by their energy, initiative, and self-denial — to save and strengthen the regime of proletarian and peasant government. This appeal met with tremendous practical success almost immediately. Thousands of workingmen proceeded toward Kerensky's forces and began digging trenches. The munition workers manned the cannon, themselves obtaining ammunition for them from various stores; requisitioned horses; brought the guns into the necessary positions and adjusted them; organized a commissary department; procured gasoline, motors, automobiles; requisitioned provisions and forage; and put the sanitary trains on a proper footing — created, in short, the entire war machinery, which we had vainly endeavored to create from above.

When scores of heavy guns reached the lines, the disposition of our soldiers changed immediately. Under cover of the artillery they were ready to repulse the Cossacks' attack. In the first lines were the sailors and Red Guards. A few officers, politically unrelated to us but sincerely attached to their regiments, accompanied their soldiers to the lines and directed their operations against Krassnov's Cossacks.

Collapse of Kerensky's Attempt

Meanwhile telegrams spread the report all over the country and abroad that the Bolshevik "adventure" had been disposed of and that Kerensky had entered Petrograd and was establishing order with an iron hand. On the other hand, in Petrograd itself, the bourgeois press, emboldened by the proximity of Kerensky's troops, wrote about the complete demoralization of the Petrograd garrison; about an irresistible advance of the Cossacks, equipped with much artillery; and predicted the imminent fall of the Smolny Institute. Our chief handicap was, as already stated, the lack of suitable mechanical accessories and of men able to direct military operations. Even those officers who had conscientiously accompanied their soldiers to the lines, declined the position of Commander-in-Chief.

After long deliberation, we hit upon the following combination: The Garrison Council selected a committee of five persons, which was entrusted with the supreme control of all operations against the counter-revolutionary forces moving on Petrograd. This committee subsequently reached an understanding with Colonel Muravief, who was in the opposition party under the Kerensky regime, and who now, on his own initiative, offered his services to the Soviet government.

On the cold night of October 30th, Muravief and I started by automobile for the lines. Wagons with provisions, forage, military supplies and artillery trailed along the road. All this was done by the workingmen of various factories. Several times our automobile was stopped on the way by Red Guard patrols who verified our permit. Since the first days of the October revolution, every automobile in town had been requisitioned, and no automobile could be ridden through the streets of the city or in the outskirts of the capital without a permit from the Smolny Institute. The vigilance of the Red Guards was beyond all praise. They stood on watch about small campfires, rifle in hand, hours at a time. The sight of these young armed workmen by the campfires in the snow was the best symbol of the proletarian revolution.

Many guns had been drawn up in position, and there was no lack of ammunition. The decisive encounter developed on this very day, between Krasnoye-Selo and Tsarskoye-Selo. After a fierce artillery duel, the Cossacks, who kept on advancing as long as they met no obstacles, hastily withdrew. They had been fooled all the time by tales of harsh and cruel acts committed by the Bolsheviki, who wished, as it were, to sell Russia to the German Kaiser. They had been assured that almost the entire garrison at Petrograd was impatiently awaiting them as deliverers. The first serious resistance completely disorganized their ranks and sealed the fate of Kerensky's entire undertaking.

The retreat of Krassnov's Cossacks enabled us to get control of the radio station at Tsarskoye-Selo. We immediately wirelessed the news of our victory over Kerensky's forces. Our foreign friends informed us subsequently that the German wireless station refused, on orders from above, to receive this wireless message.[*]

The first reaction of the German authorities to the events of October was thus one of fear — fear lest these events provoke disturbances in Germany itself. In Austria-Hungary, part of our telegram was accepted and, so far as we can tell, has been the source of information for all Europe upon the ill-starred attempt of Kerensky to recover his power and its miserable failure.

Discontent was rife among Krassnov's Cossacks. They began sending

---

[*] I cite here the text of this wireless message:

"Selo Pulkovo. General Staff 2:10 p.m. The night of October 30th-31st will go down in history. Kerensky's attempt to march counter-revolutionary forces upon the capital of the revolution has received a decisive check. Kerensky is retreating, we are advancing. The soldiers, sailors and workingmen of Petrograd have shown that they can and will, gun in hand, affirm the will and power of proletarian democracy. The bourgeoisie tried to isolate the army of the revolution and Kerensky attempted to crush it by Cossackism. Both have been frustrated.

"The great idea of the reign of a workingmen's and peasants' democracy united the ranks of the army and hardened its will. The whole country will now come to understand that the Soviet government is not a passing phenomenon, but a permanent fact of the supremacy of the workers, soldiers and peasants. Kerensky's repulse was the repulse of the middle class, the bourgeoisie and the Kornilovites. Kerensky's repulse means the affirmation of the people's rights to a free, peaceful life, to land, food and power. The Pulkovsky division, by their brilliant charge, is strengthening the cause of the proletarian and peasant revolution. There can be no return to the past. There is still fighting, obstacles and sacrifice ahead of us. But the way is open and victory assured.

"Revolutionary Russia and the Soviet Government may well be proud of their Pulkovsky division, commanded by Colonel Walden. May the names of the fallen never be forgotten. All honor to the fighters for the revolution — the soldiers and the officers who stood by the People! Long live revolutionary and Socialist Russia! In the name of the Council of People's Commissaries, L. Trotsky, Oct. 31st, 1917."

their scouts into Petrograd and even official delegates to Smolny. There they had the opportunity to convince themselves that perfect order reigned in the capital, thanks to the Petrograd garrison, which unanimously supported the Soviet government. The Cossacks' disorganization became the more acute as the absurdity of the plan to take Petrograd with some thousand horsemen dawned upon them — for the supports promised them from the front never arrived.

Krassnov's detachment withdrew to Gatchinsk, and when we started out thither the next day, Krassnov's staff were already virtually prisoners of the Cossacks themselves. Our Gatchinsk garrison was holding all the most important military positions. The Cossacks, on the other hand, though not yet disarmed, were absolutely in no position for further resistance. They wanted but one thing: to be allowed as soon as possible to return to the Don region or, at least, back to the front.

The Gatchinsk Palace presented a curious sight. At every entrance stood a special guard, while at the gates were artillery and armored cars. Sailors, soldiers and Red Guards occupied the royal apartments, decorated with precious paintings. Scattered upon the tables, made of expensive wood, lay soldiers' clothes, pipes and empty sardine boxes. In one of the rooms General Krassnov's staff had established itself. On the floor lay mattresses, caps and greatcoats.

The representative of the Revolutionary War Committee, who escorted us, entered the quarters of the General Staff, noisily dropped his rifle-butt to the floor and resting upon it, announced: "General Krassnov, you and your staff are prisoners of the Soviet authorities." Immediately armed Red Guards barred both doors. Kerensky was nowhere to be seen. He had again fled, as he had done before from the Winter Palace. As to the circumstances attending this flight, General Krassnov made a written statement on November 1st. I cite here in full this curious document.

November 1st, 1917, 19 o'clock.
About 15 o'clock today, I was summoned by the Supreme Commander-in-Chief, Kerensky. He was very agitated and nervous.

"General," said he, "you have betrayed me — your Cossacks here positively say that they will arrest me and turn me over to the sailors."

"Yes," I answered, "there is talk about it, and I know that you have no sympathizers here at all."

"But are the officers, too, of the same mind?"

"Yes, the officers are especially dissatisfied with you."

"Then, what am I to do? I'll have to commit suicide."

"If you are an honest man, you will proceed immediately to Petrograd under a flag of truce and report to the Revolutionary Committee, where you will talk things over, as the head of the Government."

"Yes, I'll do that, General!"

"I will furnish a guard for you and will ask that a sailor accompany you."

"No, anyone but a sailor. Don't you know that Dybenko is here?"

"No, I don't know who Dybenko is."

"He is an enemy of mine."

"Well, that can't be helped. When one plays for great stakes, he must be prepared to lose all."

"All right. Only I shall go at night."

"Why? That would be flight. Go calmly and openly, so that everyone can see that you are fleeing."

"Well, all right. Only you must provide for me a dependable convoy."

"All right."

I went and called out a Cossack from the 10th Don Cossack regiment, a certain Rysskov, and ordered him to appoint eight Cossacks to guard the Supreme Commander-in-Chief.

Half an hour later, the Cossacks came and reported that Kerensky had gone already — that he had fled. I gave an alarm and ordered a search for him. I believe that he cannot have escaped from Gatchinsk and must now be in hiding here somewhere.

Commanding the 3rd Corps,
Major-General Krassnov

Thus ended this undertaking.

Our opponents still would not yield, however, and did not admit that the question of government power was settled. They continued to base their hopes on the front. Many leaders of the former Soviet parties — Chernoff, Tseretelli, Avksentiev, Gotz and others — went to the front, entered into negotiations with the old army committees, and, according to newspaper reports, tried even in the camp, to form a new ministry. All this came to naught. The old army committees had lost all their significance, and intensive work was going on at the front in connection with the conferences and councils called for the purpose of reorganizing all army organizations. In these re-elections the Soviet Government was everywhere victorious.

From Gatchinsk, our divisions proceeded along the railroad further in the direction of the Luga River and Pskov. On the way, they met a few more trainloads of shock-troops and Cossacks, which had been called out by Kerensky, or which individual generals had sent over. With one of these echelons there was even an armed encounter. But most of the soldiers that were sent from the front to Petrograd declared, as soon as they met with representatives of the Soviet forces, that they had been deceived and that they would not lift a finger against the government of soldiers and workingmen.

Internal Friction

*I*n the meantime, the struggle for Soviet control spread all over the country. In Moscow, especially, this struggle took on an extremely protracted and bloody character. Perhaps not the least important cause of this was the fact that the leaders of the revolt did not at once show the necessary determination in attacking. In civil war, more than in any other, victory can be insured only by a determined and persistent course. There must be no vacillation. To engage in parleys is dangerous; merely to mark time is suicidal. We are dealing here with the masses, who have never held any power in their hands, who are therefore most wanting in political self-confidence. Any hesitation at revolutionary headquarters demoralizes them immediately. It is only when a revolutionary party steadily and resolutely makes for its goal, that it can help the toilers to overcome their century-old instincts of slavery and lead them on to victory. And only by these means of aggressive charges can victory be achieved with the smallest expenditure of energy and the least number of sacrifices.

But the great difficulty is to acquire such firm and positive tactics. The people's want of confidence in their own power and their lack of political experience are naturally reflected in their leaders, who, in their turn, find themselves subjected, besides, to the tremendous pressure of bourgeois public opinion, from above.

The liberal bourgeoisie treated with contempt and indignation the mere idea of the possibility of a working class government and gave free vent to their feelings on the subject, in the innumerable organs at their disposal. Close behind them trailed the intellectuals, who, with all their professions of radicalism and all the socialistic coating of their world-philosophy, are, in the depths of their hearts, completely steeped in slavish worship of bourgeois strength and administrative ability. All these "Socialistic" intellectuals hastily joined the Right and considered the ever-increasing strength of the Soviet government as the clear beginning of the end. After the representatives of the "liberal" professions came the petty officials, the administrative technicians — all those elements which materially and spiritually subsist on the crumbs that fall from the bourgeois table. The opposition of these elements was chiefly passive in character, especially after the crushing of the cadet insurrection; but, nevertheless, it might still seem formidable. We were being denied co-operation at every step. The government officials would either leave the Ministry or refuse to work while remaining in it. They would turn over neither the business of the department nor its money accounts. The telephone operators refused to connect us, while our messages were either held up or distorted in the telegraph offices. We could not get translators, stenographers or even copyists.

All this could not fail to create such an atmosphere as led various elements in the higher ranks of our own party to doubt whether, in the face of a boycott by bourgeois society, the toilers could manage to put the machinery of government in working order and continue in power. Opinions were voiced as to the necessity of coalition. Coalition with whom? With the liberal bourgeoisie. But an attempt at coalition with them had driven the revolution into a terrible morass. The revolt of the 25th of October was an act of self-preservation on the part of the masses after the period of impotence and treason of the leaders of coalition government. There remained for us only coalition in the ranks of so-called revolutionary democracy, that is, coalition of all the Soviet parties.

Such a coalition we did, in fact, propose from the very beginning — at the session of the Second All-Russian Council of Soviets, on the 25th of October. The Kerensky Government had been overthrown, and we suggested that the Council of Soviets take the government into its own hands. But the Right parties withdrew, slamming the door after them. And this was the best thing they could have done. They represented an insignificant section of the Council. They no longer had any following in the masses, and those classes which still supported them out of mere inertia, were coming over to our side more and more. Coalition with the Right Social-Revolutionists and the Mensheviki could not broaden the social basis of the Soviet government; and would, at the same time, introduce into the composition of this government elements which were completely disintegrated by political skepticism and idolatry of the liberal bourgeoisie. The whole strength of the new government lay in the radicalism of its program and the boldness of its actions. To tie itself up with the Chernofi and Tseretelli factions would mean to bind the new government hand and foot — to deprive it of freedom of action and thereby forfeit the confidence of the masses in the shortest possible time.

Our nearest political neighbors to the Right were the so-called "Left Social Revolutionists." They were, in general, quite ready to support us, but endeavored, nevertheless, to form a coalition Socialist government. The management of the railroad union (the so-called vikzhal), the Central Committee of the Postal Telegraph employees, and the Union of Government Officials were all against us. And in the higher circles of our own party, voices were being raised as to the necessity of reaching an understanding with these organizations, one way or another. But on what basis? All the above-mentioned controlling organizations of the old period had outlived their usefulness. They bore approximately the same relation to the entire lower personnel as did the old army committees to the masses of soldiers in the trenches. History has created a big gulf between the higher classes and the lower. Unprincipled combinations of these leaders of another day — leaders made antiquated by the revolution — were doomed to inevitable failure. It was necessary to depend wholly and confidently upon the masses in order, jointly with them, to overcome the sabotage and the aristocratic pretensions of the upper classes.

We left it to the Left Social-Revolutionists to continue the hopeless efforts for coalition. Our policy was, on the contrary, to line up the toiling lower classes against the representatives of organizations which supported the Kerensky regime. This uncompromising policy caused considerable friction and even division in the upper circles of our party. In the Central Executive Committee, the Left Social Revolutionists protested against the severity of our measures and insisted upon the necessity for compromises. They met with support on the part of some of the Bolsheviki. Three People's Commissaries gave up their portfolios and left the government. A few other party leaders sided with them in principle. This created a very deep impression in intellectual and bourgeois circles. If the Bolsheviki could not be defeated by the cadets and Krassnov's Cossacks, thought they, it is quite clear that the Soviet government must now perish as a result of internal dissension. However, the masses never noticed this dissension at all. They unanimously supported the Soviet of People's Commissaries, not only against counter-revolutionary instigators and sabotagers but also against the coalitionists and the skeptics.

The Fate of the Constituent Assembly

When, after the Korniloff episode, the ruling Soviet parties tried to smooth over their laxness toward the counter-revolutionary bourgeoisie, they demanded a speedier convocation of the Constituent Assembly. Kerensky, whom the Soviets had just saved from the too light embraces of his ally, Korniloff, found himself compelled to make compromises. The call for the Constituent Assembly was issued for the end of November. By that time, however, circumstances had so shaped themselves that there was no guarantee whatever that the Constituent Assembly would really be convoked.

The greatest degree of disorganization was taking place at the front. Desertions were increasing every day; the masses of soldiers threatened to leave the trenches, whole regiments at a time, and move to the rear, devastating everything on their way. In the villages, a general seizure of lands and landholders' utensils was going on. Martial law had been declared in several provinces. The Germans continued to advance, captured Riga, and threatened Petrograd. The right wing of the bourgeoisie was openly rejoicing over the danger that threatened the revolutionary capital. The government offices at Petrograd were being evacuated, and Kerensky's government was preparing to move to Moscow. All this made the actual convocation of the Constituent Assembly not only doubtful, but hardly even probable. From this point of view, the October revolution seems to have been the deliverance of the Constituent Assembly, as it has been the savior of the Revolution generally. When we were declaring that the road to the Constituent Assembly was not by way of Tseretelli's Preliminary Parliament, but by way of the seizure of the reigns of government by the Soviets, we were quite sincere.

But the interminable delay in convoking the Constituent Assembly was not without effect upon this institution itself. Heralded in the first days of the revolution, it came into being only after eight or nine months of bitter class and party struggle. It came too late to play a creative role. Its internal inadequacy had been predetermined by a single fact — a fact which might seem unimportant at first, but which subsequently took on tremendous importance for the fate of the Constituent Assembly.

Numerically, the principal revolutionary party in the first epoch was the party of Social-Revolutionists. I have already referred to its formlessness and variegated composition. The revolution led inevitably to the dismemberment of such of its members as had joined it under the banner of populism. The left wing, which had a following among part of the workers and the vast masses of poor peasants, was becoming more and more alienated from the rest. This wing found itself in uncompromising opposition to the party and middle bourgeois branches of Social Revolutionists. But the inertness of party organization and party tradition held back the inevitable process of cleavage. The proportional system of elections still holds full sway, as everyone knows, in party lists. Since these lists were made up two or three months before the October revolution and were not subject to change, the Left and the Right Social Revolutionists still figured in these lists as one and the same party. Thus, by the time of the October revolution — that is, the period when the Right Social Revolutionists were arresting the Left and then the Left were combining with the Bolsheviki for the overthrow of Kerensky's ministry, the old lists remained in full force; and in the elections for the Constituent Assembly the peasants were compelled to vote for lists of names at the head of which stood Kerensky, followed by those of Left Social Revolutionists who participated in the plot for his overthrow.

If the months preceding the October revolution were months of continuous gain in popular support for the Left — of a general increase in Bolshevik following among workers, soldiers and peasants — then this process was reflected within the party of Social Revolutionists in an increase of the left wing at the expense of the right. Nevertheless, on the party lists of the Social Revolutionists there was a predominance of three to one of old leaders of the right wing — of men who had lost all their revolutionary reputation in the days of coalition with the liberal bourgeoisie.

To this should be added also the fact that the elections themselves were held during the first weeks after the October revolution. The news of the change traveled rather slowly from the capital to the provinces, from the cities to the villages. The peasantry in many places had but a very vague idea of what was taking place in Petrograd and Moscow. They voted for "Land and Liberty," for their representatives in the land committees, who in most cases gathered under the banner of populism: but thereby they were voting for Kerensky and Avksentiev, who were dissolving the land committees, and arresting their members. As a result of this, there came about the strange political paradox that one of the two parties which dissolved the Constituent Assembly — the Left Social-Revolutionists — had won its representation by being on the same list of names with the party which gave a majority to the Constituent Assembly. This matter-of-fact phase of the question should give a very clear idea of the extent to which the Constituent Assembly lagged behind the course of political events and party groupings.

We must consider the question of principles.

The Principles of Democracy and Proletarian Dictatorship

*A*s Marxists, we have never been idol-worshippers of formal democracy. In a society of classes, democratic institutions not only do not eliminate class struggle, but also give to class interests an utterly imperfect expression. The propertied classes always have at their disposal tens and hundreds of means for falsifying, subverting and violating the will of the toilers. And democratic institutions become a still less perfect medium for the expression of the class struggle under revolutionary circumstances. Marx called revolutions "the locomotives of history." Owing to the open and direct struggle for power, the working people acquire much political experience in a short time and pass rapidly from one stage to the next in their development. The ponderous machinery of democratic institutions lags behind this evolution all the more, the bigger the country and the less perfect its technical apparatus.

The majority in the Constituent Assembly proved to be Social Revolutionists, and, according to parliamentary rules of procedure, the control of the government belonged to them. But the party of Right Social Revolutionists had a chance to acquire control during the entire pre-October period of the revolution. Yet, they avoided the responsibilities of government, leaving the lion's share of it to the liberal bourgeoisie. By this very course the Right Social Revolutionists lost the last vestiges of their influence with the revolutionary elements by the time the numerical composition of the Constituent Assembly formally obliged them to form a government. The working class, as well as the Red Guards, were very hostile to the party of Right Social Revolutionists. The vast majority of soldiers supported the Bolsheviki. The revolutionary element in the provinces divided their sympathies between the Left Social Revolutionists and the Bolsheviki. The sailors, who had played such an important role in revolutionary events, were almost unanimously on our side. The Right Social Revolutionists, moreover, had to

leave the Soviets, which in October — that is, before the convocation of
the Constituent Assembly — had taken the government into their own
hands. On whom, then, could a ministry formed by the Constituent
Assembly's majority depend for support? It would be backed by the
upper classes in the provinces, the intellectuals, the government officials,
and temporarily by the bourgeoisie on the Right. But such a government
would lack all the material means of administration. At such a political
center as Petrograd, it would encounter irresistible opposition from the
very start. If under these circumstances the Soviets, submitting to the
formal logic of democratic conventions, had turned the government
over to the party of Kerensky and Chernov, such a government, compromised and debilitated as it was, would only introduce temporary
confusion into the political life of the country, and would be overthrown by a new uprising in a few weeks. The Soviets decided to reduce
this belated historical experiment to its lowest terms, and dissolved the
Constituent Assembly the very first day it met.

For this, our party has been most severely censured. The dispersal of
the Constituent Assembly has also created a decidedly unfavorable
impression among the leading circles of the European Socialist parties.
Kautsky has explained, in a series of articles written with his characteristic pedantry, the interrelation existing between the Social-Revolu-
tionary problems of the proletariat and the regime of political democracy. He tries to prove that for the working class it is always expedient,
in the long run, to preserve the essential elements of the democratic
order. This is, of course, true as a general rule. But Kautsky has reduced
this historical truth to professorial banality. If, in the final analysis, it
is to the advantage of the proletariat to introduce its class struggle and
even its dictatorship, through the channels of democratic institutions,
it does not at all follow that history always affords it the opportunity
for attaining this happy consummation. There is nothing in the Marx-
ian theory to warrant the deduction that history always creates such
conditions as are most "favorable" to the proletariat.

It is difficult to tell now how the course of the Revolution would
have run if the Constituent Assembly had been convoked in its second
or third month. It is quite probable that the then dominant Social
Revolutionary and Menshevik parties would have compromised themselves, together with the Constituent Assembly, in the eyes of not only
the more active elements supporting the Soviets, but also of the more
backward democratic masses, who might have been attached, through
their expectations not to the side of the Soviets, but to that of the
Constituent Assembly. Under such circumstances the dissolution of the
Constituent Assembly might have led to new elections, in which the

party of the Left could have secured a majority. But the course of events has been different. The elections for the Constituent Assembly occurred in the ninth month of the Revolution. By that time the class struggle had assumed such intensity that it broke the formal frames of democracy by sheer internal force.

The proletariat drew the army and the peasantry after it. These classes were in a state of direct and bitter war with the Right Social Revolutionists. This party, owing to the clumsy electoral democratic machinery, received a majority in the Constituent Assembly, reflecting the pre-October epoch of the revolution. The result was a contradiction which was absolutely irreducible within the limits of formal democracy. And only political pedants who do not take into account the revolutionary logic of class relations, can, in the face of the post-October situation, deliver futile lectures to the proletariat on the benefits and advantages of democracy for the cause of the class struggle.

The question was put by history far more concretely and sharply. The Constituent Assembly, owing to the character of its majority, was bound to turn over the government to the Chernov, Kerensky and Tseretelli group. Could this group have guided the destinies of the Revolution? Could it have found support in that class which constitutes the backbone of the Revolution? No. The real kernel of the class revolution has come into irreconcilable conflict with its democratic shell. By this situation the fate of the Constituent Assembly had been sealed. Its dissolution became the only possible surgical remedy for the contradiction, which had been created, not by us, but by all the preceding course of events.

Peace Negotiations

*A*t the historic night session of the Second All-Russian Congress of the Soviets the decree on peace was adopted. (The full text is printed in the Appendix.) At that moment the Soviet government was only becoming established in the important centers of the country and there was very little confidence abroad in its power. The Soviet adopted the decree unanimously. But this seemed to many no more than a political demonstration. Those who were for a compromise preached at every opportunity that our resolution would bring no results; for, on the one hand, the German imperialists would not recognize and would not deal with us; on the other hand, our Allies would declare war upon us as soon as we should start negotiating a separate peace. Under the shadow of these predictions we took our first steps to secure a general democratic peace. The decree was adopted on the 26th of October, when Kerensky and Krassnov were at the gates of Petrograd. On the 7th of November, we addressed by wireless an invitation to our Allies and enemies to conclude a general peace. In reply the Allied Governments addressed to General Dukhonin, then commander-in-chief, through their military attaches, a communication stating that further steps to separate peace negotiations would lead to the gravest consequences. To this protest we answered the 11th of November by appealing to all the workers, soldiers and peasants. In this appeal we declared that under no circumstances would we permit our army to shed its blood under the club of the foreign bourgeoisie. We swept aside the threat of the Western imperialists and took upon ourselves the responsibility for our peace policy before the international working class. First of all, we published, in accordance with our promises, made as a matter of principle, the secret treaties and declared that we would relinquish everything in these treaties that was against the interests of the masses of the people in all countries. The capitalist governments made an attempt to make use of our disclosures against one another, but the masses of the people understood and recognized us. Not a single social patriotic publication, as far as we know, dared to protest against having all the methods of diplomacy radically changed by a government of peasants and workers; they dared not protest against us for denouncing the dishonest cunning, chicanery and cheating of the old diplomacy. We made it the task of our diplomacy to enlighten the masses of the peoples, to open their eyes to the real meaning of the policy of their governments, in order to weld them together in a common struggle and a common hatred against the bourgeois capitalist order. The German bourgeois press accused us of "dragging on" the peace negotiations; but all nations anxiously followed the discussions at Brest-Litovsk, and in this way we rendered, during the two months and a half of peace negotiations, a service to the cause of peace which was recognized even by the more honest of our enemies. The question of peace was first put before the world in a shape which made it impossible to side-track it any longer by machinations behind the scenes. On the 22nd of November a truce was signed to discontinue military activities on the entire front from the Baltic to the Black Sea. Once more we requested our Allies to join us and to conduct together with us the peace negotiations. There was no reply, though this time the Allies did not again attempt to frighten us by threats. The peace negotiations were started December 9th, a month and a half after the peace decree was adopted. The accusations of the purchased press and of the social-traitor press that we had made no attempt to agree with our Allies on a common policy was therefore entirely false. For a month and a half we kept our Allies informed about every step we made and always called upon them to become a party to the peace negotiations. Our conscience is clear before the peoples of France, Italy and Great Britain. . . . We did all in our power to get all the belligerents to join the peace negotiations. If we were compelled to start separate peace negotiations, it was not because of any fault of ours, but because of the Western imperialists, as well as those of the Russian parties, which continued predicting the approaching destruction of the workmen's and peasants' government of Russia and who persuaded the Allies not to pay serious attention to our peace initiative. But be that as it may, on the 9th of December the peace conversations were started. Our delegation made a statement of principles which set forth the basis of a general democratic peace in the exact expressions of the decree of the 26th of October (8th of November). The other side demanded that the session be broken off, and the reopening of the sessions was later, at the suggestion of Kuehlmann, repeatedly delayed. It was clear that the delegation of the Teuton Allies experienced no small difficulty in the formulation of its reply to our delegation. On the 25th of December this reply was given. The diplomats of the Teuton Allies expressed agreement with our democratic formula of peace without annexations and indemnities, on the basis of self-determination of peoples. We saw clearly that this was but pretense; but we had not expected even that they would try to pretend; because, as the French writer has said, hypocrisy is the tribute that vice pays to virtue. The fact that the German imperialists found it necessary to make this tribute to the principles of democracy, was, in our eyes, evidence that the situation of affairs within Germany was serious enough. . . . But if we, generally speaking, had no illusions concerning the love for democracy of Messrs. Kuehlmann and Czernin — we know well enough the nature of the German and Austro-Hungarian dominating classes — it must nevertheless be admitted that we had not the slightest idea of the chasm which separated the real intentions of German imperialism from those principles which were put forth on the 25th of December by Mr. von Kuehlmann as a parody on the Russian revolution — a chasm which was revealed so strikingly a few days later. Such audacity we had never expected.

Kuehlmann's reply made a tremendous impression upon the working masses of Russia. It was interpreted as a result of the fear felt by the dominant classes of the Central Empires because of the discontent and the growing impatience of the working masses of Germany. On the 28th of December there took place in Petrograd a joint demonstration of workmen and soldiers for a democratic peace. The next morning our delegation came back from Brest-Litovsk and brought those brigand demands which Mr. von Kuehlmann made to us in the name of the Central Empires as an interpretation of his "democratic" formulae.

At the first glance it may seem incomprehensible why the German diplomacy should have presented its democratic formulae if it intended within two or three days to disclose its wolfish appetite. What was it that the German diplomacy expected to bring about? At least, the theoretic discussions which developed around the democratic formulae, owing largely to the initiative of Kuehlmann himself, were not without their danger. That the diplomacy of the Central Empires could not reap many laurels in that way must have been clear beforehand to that diplomacy itself. But the secret of the conduct of the diplomacy of Kuehlmann consisted in that that gentleman was sincerely convinced of our readiness to play a four-handed game with him. His way of reasoning was approximately as follows: Russia needs peace. The Bolsheviki got the power because of their struggle for peace. The Bolsheviki desire to remain in power and this is possible for them only on condition that peace is concluded. It is true that they bound themselves to a definite democratic program of peace, but why do diplomats exist if not for the purpose of making black look white? We Germans will make it easier for the Bolsheviki by covering our plunders by democratic formulas. The Bolshevist diplomacy will have plenty of reason not to dig for the political essence of the matter, or, rather, not to expose to the entire world the contents of the enticing formulae. . . . In other words, Kuehlmann relied upon a silent agreement with us. He would return to us our fine formulas and we should give him a chance to get provinces and peoples for Germany without a protest. In the eyes of the German workers, the annexations by force would thus receive the sanction of the Russian Revolution. When during the discussions, we showed that with us, it was not a matter of empty words or of camouflaging a conspiracy concluded behind the scenes, but a matter of democratic principles for the international life of the community of nations, Kuehlmann took it as a willful and malicious breaking of the silent agreement. He would not by any means recede from the position taken in the formulas of the 25th of December. Relying upon his cunning, bureaucratic and judicial logic, he tried in the face of the entire world to show that white is in no way different from black, and it was our own perverseness which made us insist that there was such a difference. Count Czernin, the representative of Austria-Hungary, played a part in those negotiations which no one would consider inspiring or satisfactory.

He was an awkward second and upon instructions from Kuehlmann took it upon himself in all critical moments to utter the most extreme and cynical declarations. General Hoffmann brought a refreshing note into the negotiations. Showing no great sympathy for the diplomatic constructions of Kuehlmann, the General several times put his soldierly boot upon the table, around which a complicated judicial debate was developing. We, on our part, did not doubt for a single minute that just this boot of General Hoffmann was the only element of serious reality in these negotiations. The important trump in the hands of Mr. Kuehlmann was the participation in the negotiations of a delegation of the Kiev Rada. For the Ukrainian middle classes, who had seized the power, the most important factor seemed to be the "recognition" of their government by the capitalist governments of Europe. At first the Rada placed itself at the disposal of the Allied imperialists, received from them some pocket money, and immediately thereupon sent their representatives to Brest-Litovsk in order to make a bargain behind the back of the Russian people with the government of Austria-Hungary for the recognition of the legitimate birth of their government. They had hardly taken this first step on the road to "international" existence, when the Kiev diplomacy revealed the same narrow-mindedness and the same moral standards which were always so characteristic of the petty politicians of the Balkan Peninsula. Messrs. Kuehlmann and Czernin certainly had no illusions concerning the solidity of the new participant in the negotiations. But they thought, and correctly so, that the participation of the Kiev delegation complicated the game not without advantage for themselves.

At its first appearance at Brest-Litovsk, the Kiev delegation characterized Ukraine as a component part of the Russian Federated Republic that was in progress of formation. This apparently embarrassed the diplomats of the Central Empires, who considered it their main task to convert the Russian Republic into a new Balkan Peninsula. At their second appearance the delegates of the Rada declared, under dictation from the Austro-Hungarian diplomacy, that Ukraine refused to join the Russian Federation and was becoming an entirely independent republic. In order to give the reader an opportunity to get a better idea of the situation which was thus created for the Soviet power in the last moment of the peace negotiations, I think it best to reproduce here in its basic parts the address made by the author of these lines in his capacity as the People's Commissar on Foreign Affairs at the session of the Central Executive Committee on the 14th of February, 1918.

Address of the Peoples Commissar on Foreign Affairs

*C*omrades: Upon Soviet Russia has fallen the task not only to construct the new but also to recapitulate the old to a certain degree, or, rather, to a very large degree — to pay all bills, first of all the bills of the war, which has lasted three and a half years. The war put the economic power of the belligerent countries to a severe test. The fate of Russia, a poor, backward country, in a protracted war was predetermined. In the terrible collision of the military machines the determining factor, after all is said and done, is the ability of the country to adapt its industries to the military needs, to rebuild it on the shortest notice and to produce in continuously increasing quantities the weapons of destruction which are used up at such an enormous rate during this massacre of peoples. Almost every country, including the most backward, could and did have powerful weapons of destruction at the beginning of the war; that is, it obtained them from foreign countries. That is what all the backward countries did, and so did Russia. But the war speedily wears out its dead capital, demanding that it be continuously replenished. The military power of every single country drawn into the whirlpool of the world massacre was, as a matter of fact, measured by its ability to produce independently and during the war itself, its cannons and shells and the other weapons of destruction.

If the war had decided the problem of the balance of power in a very short time, Russia might conceivably have turned out to be on that side of the trenches which victory favored. But the war dragged along for a long time, and it was not an accident that it did so. The fact alone that the international politics were for the last fifty years reduced to the construction of the so-called European "balance of power," that is, to a state in which the hostile powers approximately balance one another, this fact alone was bound — when the power and wealth of the present bourgeois nations is considered — to make it a war of an extremely protracted character. That meant first of all the exhaustion of the weaker and economically less developed countries.

The most powerful country in a military sense proved to be Germany, because of the strength of the industries and because of their modern and rational construction as against the archaic construction of the German State. France, with its undeveloped state of capitalism, proved to be far behind Germany, and even such a powerful colonial power as Great Britain, owing to the conservative and routine character of the English industries, proved to be weaker than Germany. When history put before the Russian Revolution the question of the peace negotiations, we had no doubt that in these negotiations, and so long as the decisive power of the revolutionary proletariat of the world had not interfered, we should be compelled to stand the bill of three and a half years of war. There was no doubt in our minds that in the person of the German imperialism we were dealing with an opponent who was saturated with the consciousness of his immense power, which was strikingly revealed during the present war.

All the arguments made by bourgeois cliques that we might have been incomparably stronger if we had conducted these negotiations together with our allies are absolutely without foundation. In order that we might at an indefinite future date conduct negotiations together with our Allies, we should first of all have had to continue the war together with them. And if our country was weakened and exhausted, the continuation of the war, a failure to bring it to a conclusion, would have still further weakened and exhausted it. We should have had to settle the war under conditions still more unfavorable to us. In the case even that the combination of which Russia, owing to international intrigues of Czarism and the bourgeoisie, had become a part – the combination headed by Great Britain – in the case even that this combination had come out of the war completely victorious – let us for a moment admit the possibility of such a not very probable issue – even in that case, comrades, it does not mean that our country would also have come out victorious. For during further continuation of this protracted war, Russia would have become even more exhausted and plundered than now. The masters of that combination, who would concentrate in their hands the fruits of the victory, that is, Great Britain and America, would have displayed toward our country the same methods which were displayed by Germany during the peace negotiations. It would be absurd and childish to appraise the politics of the imperialistic countries from the point of view of any considerations other than those considerations of naked interests and material power. Consequently, if we, as a nation are at present weakened before the imperialism of the world, we are weakened, not because of extricating ourselves from the fiery ring of the war, having already previously extricated ourselves from the shackles of international military obligations: no! we are weakened by that very policy of the Czarists and the bourgeois classes, which we, as a revolutionary party, have always fought against before this war and during this war.

You remember, comrades, under what conditions our delegation went to Brest-Litovsk last time, right after one of the sessions of the Third All-Russian Congress of the Soviets. At that session, we reported on the state of the negotiations, and the demands of our opponents. These demands, as you remember, were really no more than masked, or, rather, half-masked annexationist aspirations at the expense of Lithuania, Courland, a part of Livonia, the Isles of Moon Sound, as well as a half-masked demand for a punitive war indemnity which we then estimated would amount to six, eight or even ten milliards of rubles. During interruption of the sessions, which continued for about ten days, a considerable disturbance took place in Austria-Hungary; strikes of masses of workers broke out, and these strikes were the first recognition of our methods of conducting peace negotiations that we met with from the proletariat of the Central Empires, as against the annexationist demands of the German militarism. We promised here no miracles but we did say that the road we were pursuing was the only road remaining to the revolutionary democracy for securing the possibility of its further development.

There is room for complaint that the proletariat of the other countries, and particularly of the Central Empires, is too slow to enter the road of open revolutionary struggle, yes, it must be admitted that the pace of its development is all too slow — but, nevertheless, there could be observed a movement in Austria-Hungary which swept the entire state and which was a direct echo of the Brest-Litovsk negotiations.

Leaving for Brest-Litovsk, it was our common opinion that there was no ground to believe that just this wave would sweep away the Austro-German militarism. If we had been convinced that this could be expected, we would gladly have given the promise that several persons demanded from us, namely, that under no circumstances would we sign a separate peace with Germany. I said at that very time, that we could not make such a promise, for it would amount to taking upon ourselves the obligation of vanquishing the German militarism. The secret of attaining such a victory was not in our possession. And inasmuch as we would not undertake the obligation to change the balance of the world powers at a moment's notice, we frankly and openly declared that revolutionary power may under certain conditions be compelled to

agree to an annexationist peace. A revolutionary power would fall short
of its high principles only in the event that it should attempt to conceal
from its own people the predatory character of the peace, but by no
means, however, in the event that the course of the struggle should
compel it to adopt such a peace.

At the same time, we indicated that we were leaving to continue
negotiations under conditions which were seemingly improving for us
and becoming worse for our enemies. We observed the movement in
Austria-Hungary, and there were signs indicating (this was made the
basis for statements by representatives of the German Social Democracy
in the Reichstag) that Germany was on the eve of similar events. We
went with this hope. During the first days of this visit to Brest-Litovsk
the wireless brought us from Vilna the first news that in Berlin an
enormous strike movement was developing; this movement as well as
that of Austria-Hungary was directly connected with the course of
negotiations in Brest. However, as is often the case, by reason of the
dialectic of the class struggle, just this conspicuous beginning of the
proletarian rising, which surpassed anything Germany had ever seen,
was bound to push the property classes to a closer consolidation and
to greater hostility against the proletariat. The German dominating
classes are saturated with a sufficiently strong instinct of self-preservation to understand that concessions in such an exigency as they were
in, under the pressure of the masses of their own people — concessions
however small — would amount to capitulation before the idea of the
revolution. That is why, after the first moment of perplexity and panic,
the time when Kuehlmann deliberately dragged out the negotiations by
minor and formal questions, had passed — as soon as the strikes were
disposed of, as soon as he came to the conclusion that for the time
being no imminent danger threatened his masters, he again changed
front and adopted a tone of unlimited self-confidence and aggression.

Our negotiations were complicated by the participation of the Kiev
Rada. We called attention to this last time, too. The delegation from the
Kiev Rada appeared at a time when the Rada represented a fairly strong
organization in the Ukraine and when the way out of the war had not
yet been predetermined. Just at that time, we made the Rada an official
offer to conclude a definite treaty with us, making as one of the
conditions of such a treaty the following demand: that the Rada declare
Kaledin and Korniloff to be counter-revolutionists and put no hin-
drance in the way of our waging war on these two leaders. The delegation
from the Kiev Rada arrived, just when we hoped to reach an understanding with it on these matters. We declared that as long as the people
of the Ukraine recognized the Rada, we considered its independent

participation in these negotiations permissible. But with the further development of events in Russian territory and in the Ukraine, and the more the antagonism between the Ukrainian masses and the Rada increased, the greater became the Rada's readiness to conclude any kind of treaty with the governments of the Central Empires, and, if need be, to drag German imperialism into the internal affairs of the Russian Republic, in order to support the Rada against the Russian revolution.

On the 9th day of February (N.S.) we learned that the peace negotiations carried on behind our backs between the Rada and the Central Powers, had been signed. The 9th of February happened to be the birthday of Leopold of Bavaria, and, as is the custom in monarchical countries, the triumphant historical act was timed — with or without the consent of the Kiev Rada for this festive day. General Hoffmann had a salute fired in honor of Leopold of Bavaria, having previously asked permission to do so of the Kiev delegation, since by the treaty of peace Brest-Litovsk had been ceded to Ukraine.

Events had taken such a turn, however, that at the time General Hoffmann was asking permission for a military salute, the Kiev Rada had but very little territory left outside of Brest-Litovsk. On the strength of the telegrams we had received from Petrograd, we officially made it known to the Central Powers' delegation that the Kiev Rada no longer existed, a circumstance which certainly had some bearing on the course of the peace negotiations. We suggested to Count Czernin that his representatives accompany our officers into Ukrainian territory to ascertain whether the Kiev Rada existed or not. Czernin seemed to welcome this suggestion, but when we asked him if this meant that the treaty made with the Kiev delegation would not be signed before the return of his own mission, he hesitated and promised to ask Kuehlmann about it. Having inquired, he sent us an answer in the negative.

This was on February 8th. By the 9th, they had to sign the treaty. This could not be delayed, not only on account of Leopold's birthday, but for a more important reason, which Kuehlmann undoubtedly explained to Czernin: "If we should send our representatives into the Ukraine just now, they might really convince themselves that the Rada does not exist; and then we shall have to face a single All-Russian delegation which would spoil our prospects in the negotiations. . . ." By the Austro-Hungarian delegation we were advised to put principle aside and to place the question on a more practical plane. Then the German delegation would be disposed to concessions. . . . It was unthinkable that the Germans should decide to continue the war over, say, the Moon Islands, if you put this demand in concrete form.

We replied that we were ready to look into such concessions as their

German colleagues were prepared to make. "So far we have been con-
tending for the self-determination of the Lithuanians, Poles, Livonians,
Letts, Esthonians, and other peoples; and on all these issues you have
told us that such self-determination is out of the question. Now let us
see what your plans are in regard to the self-determination of another
people – the Russians; what designs and plans of a military strategic
nature are behind your seizure of the Moon Islands. For these islands,
as an integral part of an independent Estonian Republic, or as a
possession of the Federated Russian Republic would have only a defen-
sive military importance, while in the hands of Germany they would
assume offensive significance, menacing the most vital centers of our
country, and especially Petrograd."

But, of course, Hoffmann would make no concessions whatsoever.
Then the hour for reaching a decision had come. We could not declare
war, for we were too weak. The army had lost all of its internal ties. In
order to save our country, to overcome this disorganization, it was
imperative to establish the internal coherence of the toilers. This psychological tie can only be created by constructive work in factory, field
and workshop. We had to return the masses of laborers, who had been
subjected to great and intense suffering – who had experienced catas-
trophes in the war – to the fields and factories, where they must find
themselves again and get a footing in the labor world, and rebuild
internal discipline. This was the only way to save the country, which
was now atoning for the sins of Czarism and the bourgeoisie. We had
to get out of the war and withdraw the army from the slaughter house.
Nevertheless, we threw this in the face of the German militarism: The
peace you are forcing down our throats is a peace of aggression and
robbery. We cannot permit you, Messrs. Diplomats, to say to the
German workingmen: "You have characterized our demands as avari-
cious, as annexationist. But look, under these very demands we have
brought you the signature of the Russian revolution." Yes, we are weak,
we cannot fight at present. But we have sufficient revolutionary courage
to say that we shall not willingly affix our signature to the treaty which
you are writing with the sword on the body of living peoples. We refused
to affix our signature. I believe we acted properly, comrades.

I do not mean to say, friends, that a German advance upon Russia
is out of the question. It were too rash to make such an assertion in
view of the great strength of the German imperialistic party. But I do
believe that the stand we have taken in the matter has rendered it far
more difficult for German militarism to advance upon us. What would
happen if it should advance? To this there is but one thing to say: If it
is possible in our country, a country completely exhausted and in a state

of desperation, to raise the spirits of the more revolutionary energetic elements; if a struggle in defense of our Revolution and the territory comprised within it is still possible, then this is the case only as a result of our abandoning the war and refusing to sign the peace treaty.

The Second War and the Signing of Peace

During the first few days following the breaking off of negotiations the German government hesitated, not knowing what course to pursue. The politicians and diplomats evidently thought that the principal objects had been accomplished and that there was no reason for coveting our signatures. The military men were ready, in any event, to break through the lines drawn by the German Government at Brest-Litovsk. Professor Krigge, the advisor of the German delegation, told a member of our delegation that a German invasion of Russia under the existing conditions was out of the question. Count Mirbach, then at the head of the German missions at Petrograd, went to Berlin with the assurance that an agreement concerning the exchange of prisoners of war had been satisfactorily reached. But all this did not in the least prevent General Hoffmann from declaring on the fifth day after the Brest-Litovsk negotiations had been broken off — that the armistice was over, ante-dating the seven-day period from the time of the last Brest-Litovsk session. It were really out of place to dilate here on the moral indignation caused by this piece of dishonesty. It fits in perfectly with the general state of diplomatic and military morality of the ruling classes.

The new German invasion developed under circumstances most fatal for Russia. Instead of the week's notice agreed upon, we received notice only two days in advance. This circumstance intensified the panic in the army which was already in state of chronic dissolution. Resistance was almost unthinkable. The soldiers could not believe that the Germans would advance after we had declared the state of war at an end. The panicky retreat paralyzed the will even of such individual detachments as were ready to make a stand. In the workingmen's quarters of Petrograd and Moscow, the indignation against the treacherous and truly murderous German invasion reached a pitch of greatest intensity. In these alarming days and nights, the workers were ready to enlist in the army by the ten thousand. But the matter of organizing lagged far behind. Isolated tenacious detachments full of enthusiasm became convinced themselves of their instability in their first serious clashes with German regulars. This still further lowered the country's spirits. The old army had long ago been hopelessly defeated and was going to pieces, blocking all the roads and byways. The new army, owing to the country's general exhaustion, the fearful disorganization of industries and the means of transportation, was being got together too slowly. Distance was the only serious obstacle in the way of the German invasion.

The chief attention of the Austro-Hungarian government was centered on the Ukraine. The Rada, through its delegation, had appealed to the governments of the Central Empires for direct military aid against the Soviets, which had by that time completely defeated the Ukrainians. Thus did the petty-bourgeois democracy of the Ukraine, in its struggle against the working class and the destitute peasants, voluntarily open the gates to foreign invasion.

At the same time, the Svinhufvud government was seeking the aid of German bayonets against the Finnish proletariat. German militarism, openly and before the whole world, assumed the role of executioner of the peasant and proletarian revolution in Russia.

In the ranks of our party hot debates were being carried on as to whether or not we should, under these circumstances, yield to the German ultimatum and sign a new treaty, which — and this no one doubted — would include conditions incomparably more onerous than those announced at Brest-Litovsk. The representatives of the one view held that just now, with the German intervention in the internal war of the Russian Republic, it was impossible to establish peace for one part of Russia and remain passive, while in the South and in the North, German forces would be establishing a regime of bourgeois dictatorship. Another view, championed chiefly by Lenin, was that every delay, even the briefest breathing spell, would greatly help the internal stabilization and increase the Russian powers of resistance. After the whole country and the whole world had come to know of our absolute helplessness against foreign invasion at this time, the conclusion of peace would everywhere be understood as an act forced upon us by the cruel law of disproportionate forces. It would be childish to argue from the standpoint of abstract revolutionary ethics. The point is not to die with honor but to achieve ultimate victory. The Russian Revolution wants to survive, must survive, and must by every means at its disposal avoid fighting an uneven battle and gain time, in the hope that the Western revolutionary movement will come to its aid.

German imperialism is still engaged in a fierce annexationist struggle with English and American militarism. Only because of this is the conclusion of peace between Russia and Germany at all possible. We must fully avail ourselves of this situation. The welfare of the Revolution is the highest law. We should accept the peace which we are unable to reject; we must secure a breathing spell to be utilized for intensive work within the country and, especially, for the creation of an army.

At the conference of the Communist party as well as at the Fourth Conference of the Soviet, the peace partisans triumphed. They were joined by many of those who in January considered it impossible to sign the Brest-Litovsk treaty. "Then," said they, "our signature would have been looked upon by the English and French workingmen as a shameful capitulation, without an attempt to fight. Even the base insinuations of the Anglo-French chauvinists to the secret compact between the Soviet Government and the Germans, might in case that treaty had been signed find credence in certain circles of European laborers. But after we had refused to sign the treaty, after a new German invasion, after our attempt to resist it, and after our military weakness had become painfully obvious to the whole world, after all this, no one dare to reproach us for surrendering without a fight."

The Brest-Litovsk treaty, in its second enlarged edition, was signed and ratified.

In the meantime, the executioners were doing their work in Finland and the Ukraine, menacing more and more the most vital centers of Great Russia. Thus the question of Russia's very existence as an independent country is henceforth inseparably connected with the question of the European revolution.

Conclusion

*W*hen our party took over the government, we knew in advance what difficulties we had to contend with. Economically the country had been exhausted by the war to the very utmost. The revolution had destroyed the old administrative machinery and could not yet create anything to take its place. Millions of workers had been wrested from their normal nooks in the national economy of things, declassified, and physically shattered by the three years' war. The colossal war industries, carried on on an inadequately prepared national foundation, had drained all the lifeblood of the people; and their demobilization was attended with extreme difficulties. The phenomena of economic and political anarchy spread throughout the country. The Russian peasantry had for centuries been held together by barbarian national discipline from below and iron-Czarist rule from above. Economic development had undermined the former, the revolution destroyed the latter. Psychologically, the revolution meant the awakening of a sense of human personality among the peasantry. The anarchic manifestations of this awakening are but the inevitable results of the preceding oppression. A new order of things, an order based on the workers' own control of industry, can come only through gradual and internal elimination of the anarchic manifestations of the revolution.

On the other hand, the propertied classes, even though deprived of political power, will not relinquish their advantages without a fight. The Revolution has brought to a head the question of private property in land and the tools of production — that is, the question of vital significance to the exploiting classes. Politically this means ceaseless, secret or open civil war. In its turn, civil war inevitably nourishes anarchical tendencies within the workingmen's movement. With the disorganization of industries, of national finances, of the transportation and provisioning systems, prolonged civil strife thus sets up tremendous difficulties in the way of constructive organizing work. Nevertheless, the Soviet Government can look the future in the face with perfect confidence. Only a careful inventory of all the country's resources; only a rational organization of industries — an organization born of one general plan; only wise and careful distribution of all the products, can save the country. And this is Socialism. Either a complete descent to colonial status or a Socialist resurrection — these are the alternatives before which our country finds itself.

The war has undermined the soil of the entire capitalistic world. Herein lies our unconquerable strength. The imperialistic ring that is pressing around us will lie burst asunder by the proletarian revolution. We do not doubt this for a minute, anymore than we doubted during our decades of underground struggle the inevitableness of the downfall of Czarism.

To struggle, to unite our forces, to establish industrial discipline and a Socialist regime, to increase the productivity of labor, and to press on in the face of all obstacles — this is our mission. History is working in our favor. The proletarian revolution will flare up, sooner or later, both in Europe and America, and will bring emancipation not only to the Ukraine, Poland, Lithuania, Courland, and Finland, but also to all suffering humanity.